YES, AND!

HARNESSING THE POWER OF IMPROVISATION TO
TRANSFORM YOUR LIFE AND WORK

By
Mary Jane Pories

Address all inquiries to:

Fishladder Press
3510 Reeds Lake Blvd.SE
Grand Rapids, MI 49506-2437
www.fishladder.net

Ordering Information:

Special discounts are available on quantity purchases by corporations, associations, educators, and others. For details, contact the publisher at the above listed address.

U.S. trade bookstores and wholesalers:
Please contact Fishladder Press Tel: (616) 540-6595 or email: info@fishladder.net.

First Printing: 2014

ISBN: 978-0-9859017-2-1 (hc)
ISBN 978-009859017-0-7 (sc)
ISBN 978-0-9859017-1-4 (e)

Library of Congress Control Number: 2014910625

Cover Copyright © Fishladder Inc.
Cover design by Jude Aldren, Key Jude Designs
Book design and production by Fishladder Press
www.fishladder.net
Illustrations © 2014 Walter J. Pories
Photo The Scream by Mary Jane Pories
Author photograph by Gayla Fox Photography

Disclaimer: *Some names and identifying details have been changed to protect the privacy of individuals.*

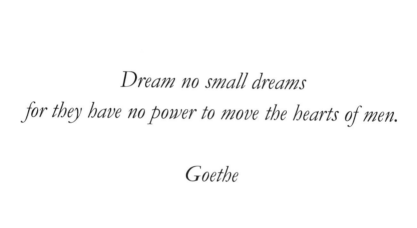

Dream no small dreams
for they have no power to move the hearts of men.

Goethe

Dedication

To Eric Black
One of the hardest working improvisers I've
known who tirelessly prepared for those brilliant,
raucous, spontaneous moments on stage
and left us too soon.

Contents

How to Use This Book

Every morning I jump out of bed and step on a landmine.
The landmine is me.
Ray Bradbury

According to Harvard researcher Daniel Goleman, author of *Emotional Quotient*, *Primal Leadership*, and *Social Intelligence*, laughter is the fastest way to create a bond between two people or a group. When we laugh, we share an experience. The experience gives us something in common.

That shared experience is what improvisation is all about. The laughter disarms us. Barriers go down and collaboration goes up. We let go of egos and listen to each other.

We don't tell jokes. We find the funny together. We tell it like it is. We don't laugh at someone else's expense. And that's what is wonderful about it. Improvisation often results in humor, but comedy is not the real goal.

I learned this spending a week with Paul Sills in Door County, Wisconsin. His mother, Viola Spolin, found the magic in this work for children. Paul took the work to the stage as the first director

> **Games** are the most elevated form of investigation.
> Albert Einstein.

of *The Second City*. He was careful to make the distinction between improv — the short form games found in comedy clubs — and improvisation — the exploration of the entirety of the human condition. Improvisation goes beyond the comedy to bring us the totality of angst, absurdity, and brilliance that are a part of everyday life. It's theater on your feet.

Don't get me wrong. There's lots of humor in improvisation. Because great improvisation tells the truth about the human condition, there's lots of comedy.

Laughter is the result of surprise. A comment or event interrupts an established pattern and we suddenly see something we've seen a gazillion times before in a new way. From that, we gain a new insight, perspective, or solution. Frankly, this is what makes the work so exciting, so mysterious and, yes, so entertaining.

Improvised entertainment takes place on a stage in front of a live audience. The secret is that each performance takes a lot of work. Don't forget, it's a business. To be profitable, theaters have to sell shows. This requires nimble performers, expert at their craft, performing a well-planned, prepared, and rehearsed show. Producers can't afford to "wing it" in the hope that the show is entertaining.

To keep the audience in their seats and leave them wanting more, improvisers rehearse, write, watch recorded versions of improv sets and performances, watch other shows, read about improvisation, and do whatever else it takes to excel in the craft. They prepare for those few precious moments with their patrons. The entertainers can't afford to "wing it."

Improvisers prepare out of respect for those who attend and to keep their jobs. They practice to strengthen skills and advance careers. The more they prepare, the more effortless it looks. That's how they create these seemingly spontaneous unforgettable performances.

And this is what we can learn from them.

Learning how they prepare to perform at this high level can help you meet the needs of customers, sell services, and grow your business. Once it's in your bones, it can do the same in your personal life. With improvisation, you become a resilient problem-solver. You think on your feet. You face the unexpected with calm, clarity, and creativity.

This book is your guide to applying the tools of improvisation in the workplace. It will help you make the most of each moment. Rather than thinking, "I wish I'd said...," you can be ready for anything.

This book provides instruction, stories, examples, and exercises that will help you master the skills and apply them immediately. It will improve business practices. But, be ready for more. Improvisation is transformative. Its power can make the world a better place.

Cultivate the Environment

To make it work, you need the right environment. Just like a productive garden is rooted in fertile soil, you need to ensure you have the right mixture ripe for the cultivation of a culture of improvisation.

Demand honesty of yourself and others. Improvisation requires a rigorous attentiveness to honesty. Truth **DEMAND** telling. Like good soil, which contains a certain **HONESTY** amount of manure, this means we tell the truth about the good and the bad. We take the blinders off and take a good look at ourselves first, then others. Output reflects the quality of the input. The soil we seek contains the nutrients that come from processing what comes in and dealing with it in an honest way. We can't be afraid of conflict. In fact, an absence of conflict is indicative of dishonesty. We don't want battles but we do want honest contributions. We want people to speak up. We want the diversity of opinion — the intensity that leads to transformed relationships and brilliant innovation.

When we don't trust the people around us, we hide our mistakes. We pretend everything's going well. We **ALLOW FOR** omit critical information. We blame others. Cultures **MISTAKES** that allow for mistakes understand that mistakes invite critical analysis. A willingness to admit you're not perfect creates connections between people. Leaders become more vulnerable and can then hear the good ideas of their people. We don't continue to repeat our errors because we've had the opportunity to learn from them. We do not reward carelessness. That's different. We reward people who are doing their best to make things work and yet, despite those best efforts, something goes awry. They "fail."

Improvisers do not believe in mistakes. They try to avoid the word at all costs. There are only choices that need to be justified. There are only decisions that need to be understood and then built upon for the greatest resolution. Events that require an uncharted response.

MAKE EACH OTHER LOOK GREAT When a scene is going poorly on stage, I do not have the luxury of standing back and thinking to myself, "Wow. I'm sure glad I'm not in that scene. It's awful. Poor saps." My responsibility, no matter what, is to make the other players look great. That means, for starters, I'm attentive to their choices even when I'm not in the scene. I can't assume that because I'm not in it, it's not my responsibility. That's how we get silos in the workplace. Next, I'm required to assess what I can do to make them look great. Sometimes I should enter the scene. Sometimes I should stay out of it. Sometimes I can be a prop. The choice, however, should never be about me. It can't be that I'm looking for the limelight, wanting attention, trying to get the promotion. My thoughts need to be for the good of the team.

So, start by determining what you can do to create this environment. What needs to be changed? What can you do to change it?

When Ray Bradbury said, "Every morning I jump out of bed and step on a landmine. The landmine is me," he reminds us, we are our own worst landmines. We need to get out of our own way to discover a new way. Doing things the way we've always done them before is a dead end. Unless we change, we're going to be looking at a lot of behinds.

If you want to become more visionary, learn to improvise. If you want to think on your feet, learn to improvise. If you want to become more agile in the face of change, learn to improvise.

Here are just a few things you will get better at:

- Listening and getting others to listen to you
- Saying what you mean
- Solving problems with speed and agility
- Engaging teamwork
- Finding the funny
- Leading confidently
- Innovating audaciously

Every day is a new adventure and if you're not ready for it, someone else will be.

It's time to: Quit winging it and improvise!

P.S. You may feel foolish at times. This work is humbling and requires vulnerability — a trait familiar in the best leaders.

I invite you to make a fool of yourself...in the best possible way.

PLAY LIST
→ Tell the truth
→ Allow for mistakes
→ Make each other look great

Foreword

It is humbling to have been asked to write a foreword to this forward-thinking book. I'm a designer who long ago made the shift from designing things to designing situations. My joy is in connecting interesting people with possibilities for their growth and seeing them succeed. My more than 40 years in the design world has included such opportunities as being the VP of Corporate Communications at Herman Miller; developing Design West Michigan, an advocacy group for advancing design as an economic building block; and working with Kendall College of Art and Design to develop new degrees and learning opportunities. During the development of a BFA in Collaborative Design, I was introduced to Mary Jane Pories and together we recognized how a class on improvisation would be valuable to help creative individuals learn how to communicate better. That class now exists and has helped many students become more secure in their communication capabilities early in their careers.

Early in my career, I heard someone say "Most business problems are communication problems," and "the most creative results come from multiple disciplines working on a common problem." While I can't attribute these words, they are tenants I believe. What's been difficult is finding a way to validate those beliefs and/or provide instruction for practice and application. Mary Jane's careful writings and thoughtful directions provide a guidebook to help accomplish and lead in such collaborations, while gaining the value from different thinkers. And yes, she clearly gives evidence to the process and importance of good communications. Her shared stories from real-life experiences provide examples we all can learn from.

Today, the world of work requires greater flexibility than ever before. We must develop an ability to respond to ever-changing needs, adjust to unforeseen changes in the marketplace, or respond to circumstances out of anyone's control. Interpersonal communications among the teams that must deal with such change requires the skills to move quickly, gain a shared understanding of the situation, and collectively move forward and adapt. It is my belief that the skills of improvisation are needed to facilitate such change.

Improvisation is often reduced merely to comedic entertainment, which it certainly is. This book, however, shows how those same learned skills can help advance us all into more productive and enjoyable experiences, both professionally and personally.

This is a textbook, a guidebook, and yes, a self-help book, while being a good read. Mary Jane's experiences from her time spent at *The Second City* provide real-life examples of learning. Imagine how great it would be if the folks we interact with were skilled in improvisation. Think of business conversations that might actually achieve innovation, such as new products and services from the fertile minds that too often don't get the chance to express, share, and grow. And yes, after reading this book, we should each be a catalyst to help make that happen.

With a firm belief that collaboration is a key to the future of our economy and social well-being, this book can help accomplish that vision. Enjoy.

John R. Berry
Executive Director, Design West Michigan and author of
Herman Miller: The Purpose of Design, published by Rizzoli.

Preface

A fixed attitude is a closed door.
Viola Spolin

My fear of heights destroyed the cartilage in both of my knees — indirectly, of course. A beginning hiker, with new equipment and little sense, I decided to tackle the Grand Canyon as my first attempt. The decision required a completely unrealistic and overly confident assessment of my abilities.

After all, I told myself, the canyon is just a big hole. How hard can it be? I laced up my brand new hiking boots and cut the tags off my backpack. I stuffed in the essentials, adding a collapsible chair, bathroom slippers, a couple books, and paints. My backpack weighed more than 40 pounds — too much for my small frame, as I discovered on the third switchback. According to my research, after the trip, I should have been carrying no more than 25 pounds.

My best friend planned for our trip. She was prepared. I was not. My lack of planning and a few surprises left me a changed person.

Our departure time from the South Rim of the Grand Canyon was to be in the cool of the morning. Because of the desert sun, the guidebooks suggested a 5 a.m. start to beat the heat of the day. For reasons never completely clarified, the park ranger from the South Kaibab Trail informed us that our start time had been delayed. Five hours later, the ranger recited our final instructions, peppering them with horror stories of death and dehydration. We peered over the edge as he talked. The trail itself appeared striking and brutal — a dramatic beauty crying out for my demise. I was sure my camera would be the only record of my last moments alive.

Within yards of leaving the comfort of the park office, what little bravado I had left gave way to terror, and my knees locked. I looked more like a tiny replica of Frankenstein than an agile, healthy hiker.

On my right, a wall littered with smirking vegetation. On my left, a sheer drop off, advertised repeatedly by bits of kamikaze rubble, freely leaping off the toe of my boot and then gone. I hiked down to the Colorado River, straight-legged and leaning hard into the mountain.

With my knees locked, my pace slowed and I fell far behind my hiking partner. Worst of all, I locked out the grandeur and beauty of the Grand Canyon. I focused instead on my knees, the dusty path in front of me, and my impending death. Moving so awkwardly, I slid and stumbled. Hikers twice my age sailed past me and were cooling their feet in the river long before I reached its banks. By the time I did arrive, I was sweaty, miserable, and frustrated knowing I had become my own greatest obstacle.

My work in improvisation also began in resistance.

In the summer of 1994, I was invited to audition for a local improv troupe. I immediately said, "No." I'd seen improvisation and I thought the whole idea was stupid. Why would anyone want to get up in front of an audience without a script and make a complete fool of herself?

Not that I was a stranger to foolish behavior. It's just that if anything, I was trying to look less foolish, not more.

They persisted and I gave in. I needed the friends. I gave in thinking, "I'll go to one rehearsal. What can it hurt? I'll watch them for a bit, graciously decline any overtures to get involved, and make it home in time for my favorite crime show.

So, that's what I did. I showed up ready to watch. I stood off to the side. Amazed at their energy and creativity, I was even more sure it wasn't for me. I folded my arms. I wanted to make sure they understood my body language. "Have fun but don't you dare ask me to play."

I knew I would never be able to think that fast on my feet. I liked traditional theater with a director who handed me a script and told me where to stand. I needed someone to tell me what to say, when to say it, and when to keep quiet. This was too loose and too scary.

Still I was curious. I asked the leader of the troupe, "How can they think this stuff up so fast? Where do they get these ideas?" His response, "They say 'Yes, And!' to any initiation."

"I don't get it."

"Any suggestion, no matter how bizarre, the other person agrees to it and adds to it."

"That's it?"

"Yup. Try it." And with that, he pushed me into the scene. I don't recommend pushing people into things but he knew me well enough to know that was the only way I'd ever try it. He was right.

That was almost 20 years ago. I've been improvising ever since — on stage but also using it in my business and, honestly, everywhere else.

My discovery that night: we can do anything we want with a moment. We can create anything we want by just changing our mindset. And all we need is each other and a willing attitude.

Like many people I work with today, I resisted the unfamiliar. And with good reason. Improvisation seems to embody everything most of us are trying to avoid: uncertainty, ambiguity, the unknown.

But really, the opposite is true.

Through years of study and practice, I know that improvisation gives me sure footing in uncertain times. Without it, I am brittle, resistant, and frightened. With it, I'm ready for anything.

Each day that you are fortunate to wake up, you meet face-to-face with the unexpected. At home and at work, others around you are doing the same. Many times, you react well and breathe a sigh of relief. "Wow. I made it through that one." But you and I both know that we'd like to do more than "make it through." We'd like to respond with confidence. We'd like to be able to keep our cool, flash through the options, and make the best possible decision at the time. We'd like to be more prepared.

Assuming we agree that we all improvise every day, why try to avoid the unexpected? Better yet, why not be more proactive? Instead of resorting to being a victim of surprise, why not plan for the unexpected?

It's time to stop living in denial. Expect things to go awry. Expect your company to surpass or disappoint. Expect your loved ones to do the same — thrill and disappoint.

If we're willing to forecast a budget or set policy for risk management, why not use those same skills to anticipate what might suddenly invade the moment and take us on a journey.

Dispelling the Myth

Before we begin, it's only fair that we understand the myth surrounding improvisation. Many, unfortunately, are under the impression that improvisation is synonymous with "winging it." If you're one of those people, it's not hard to discover why you're working under that assumption.

For starters, every dictionary uses a similar, if not identical, definition. Here's the one from the *American Heritage Dictionary*:

im·pro·vise

To invent, compose, or perform with little or no preparation.[1] It doesn't stop here. The expression, "winging it," derives from the phrase "on a wing and a prayer." The military used this term to refer to aircraft they hoped, rather than expected, would return to the base.

The theatrical expression refers to impromptu performances given by actors who hurriedly learned their lines while waiting in the wings and then received prompts from there. The phrase dates from the late 19th century with the verb "to wing," first defined in an 1885 edition of *Stage* magazine.

Improvisers themselves need to take responsibility as well. In our effort to be accessible, we've downplayed the effort required to master the skills. Even one of my heroes, Charna Halpern, in her much-revered book, *Truth in Comedy*, leads with "True improvisation is getting on-stage and performing without any preparation or planning."

Or sometimes, in our effort to appear awesome, we perpetuate the myth. Michelangelo gives us a perfect example of this. Many of us know the following quotation describing his work process, "I saw the angel in the marble and carved until I set him free."

But another quote provides us a deeper understanding of the real talent and work behind his masterpieces. He also said, "If you knew how much work went into it, you wouldn't call it genius."

If we're honest with ourselves, this is more often the reason we want others to think we're "winging it." We yearn to awe and amaze those around us. If the perception is that we are extraordinarily talented, we stand out in a crowd. To do this, we take pride in "just showing up." We boast that we gave the talk, answered the question, or led the meeting "without any planning or preparation."

---

[1]   Improvise. *The American Heritage® Dictionary of the English Language, Fourth Edition.* Houghton Mifflin Company, 2000. Updated in 2009.

Of course, we are not telling the whole truth. The whole truth is that, along with passion and talent, if we want great results, we need to do the hard work.

Granted, it is amazing when, in the face of the unexpected, we somehow say or do just the right thing. We respond with resilience and grace. We surprise ourselves with our insights, our intellect.

The problem is that by perpetuating the myth of "winging it," we are incorrect; we encourage blatant disrespect for others. To show up for a talk or meeting unprepared is a careless approach to other people's time. They prepared, they are ready, and we, because of hubris or carelessness, just show up.

Whenever possible, we ought to revere the gift of other people's time and attention and prepare as thoroughly as possible. Surprisingly, that's exactly what improvisers do for the stage. They plan, prepare, and practice. At *The Second City*, when working on a new show, we performed seven shows a week, five improv sets a week, rehearsed 22 hours a week, and then got together with scene partners to write and practice. We didn't wing it.

We also didn't know what exactly would happen on stage until the actual performance. Plenty of nights, because of a missing prop, a bad transmission, or a drunken audience member, things didn't go as planned.

This is true for you as well. You plan, prepare, and practice and, sometimes, nothing goes as planned. Is that "winging it?"

Not to me. Your ability to respond so well that you even surprise yourself is the culmination of all those times you did plan, prepare, and practice. Malcolm Gladwell refers to mastery in his book, *Outliers*. This is when those 10,000 hours of practice finally pay off. You're ready for anything.

Captain Sullenberger

Perhaps you recall January 15, 2009, when the world applauded the heroic efforts of US Airways pilot Chesley "Sully" Sullenberger. His Airbus 360 hit a flock of birds shortly after taking off from New York's LaGuardia Airport, disabling both engines. News reports led us to believe that his quick thinking allowed him to improvise and safely ditch the plane in the icy Hudson River, sparing the lives of all on-board.

We watched in awe as passengers huddled onto both wings to wait for the nearby ferryboats and barges to pluck them from the sinking plane. It was a remarkable example of calm after the storm.

And our first question was, "How did Sully do it?"

To say he was "winging it" is untrue (and only mildly amusing as a pun). His ability to react so quickly and so well in the moment, to improvise his way to safety, had everything to do with years of planning, preparing, and practicing the default behaviors it called for.

Sully had 40 years of experience, logging 20,000 flight hours in jets, planes, and gliders. He already was an established speaker on aviation safety and, according to his wife, even when he is a passenger on a plane, follows the safety card as the attendants recite them before takeoff. He plans, he prepares, and he practices. Nothing is accidental. He is the consummate improviser.

Bill Clinton

Despite your political leaning, for most people, Bill Clinton is widely recognized as a great orator. So, I like many others, was not surprised when he assumed the podium and delivered one of the most memorable speeches at the Democratic Convention in Charlotte, NC, in 2012. What caught my attention was the headline on National Public Radio. They referred to him as "Improviser in Chief." They went on to say,

> "As president and as a candidate, Bill Clinton was known for sometimes winging it — even in major speeches. In 1994, Clinton famously spoke from memory for a time when the wrong version of his State of the Union address appeared on his teleprompter.
>
> "That was the same Bill Clinton who spoke to Democratic convention delegates for nearly 50 minutes Wednesday night — adding about 2,300 words to a speech that started with 3,200 words of prepared text."

The *Atlantic Wire* also picked up the story in "What Bill Clinton Wrote vs. What Bill Clinton Said" by Dashell Bennett.[2] The story begins,

> "If you were following any journalists on Twitter last night, one of the most remarked upon aspects of Bill Clinton's nomination speech was how liberally he deviated from the prepared text. What was handed out to the media was four pages of single-spaced, small font text, but — as an exasperated TelePrompTer operator found out — that was really just a guideline to what Clinton actually wanted to say during his 49-minute address. We decided to compare the two versions to see how one of the great speechmakers of his era goes about his business.
>
> Most experienced public speakers know how to deviate and alter and add flourishes to their prepared remarks on the fly, but few do it as well as Clinton."

The writers then provide readers with a visual showing the written speech compared to what he actually said while standing at the podium. Here's a sample with "Clinton's insertions in italics and his deletions struck out":

> *And so here's what I want to say to you, and here's what I want the people at home to think about.* When times are tough, *and people are frustrated and angry*

---

2   Bennett, Dashell. "What Bill Clinton Wrote vs. What Bill Clinton Said." September 6, 2012. *The Atlantic Wire.*

and hurting and uncertain, the politics of constant conflict may be good
~~politics but in the real world, cooperation works better.~~ *But what is
good politics does not necessarily work in the real world. What works in the real
world is cooperation. What works in the real world is cooperation, business and
government, foundations and universities. Ask the mayors who are here. Los
Angeles is getting green and Chicago is getting an infrastructure bank because
Republicans and Democrats are working together to get it. They didn't check
their brains at the door. They didn't stop disagreeing, but their purpose was to
get something done. Now, why is this true? Why does cooperation work better
than constant conflict? Because* ~~After all,~~ *nobody's right all the time, and
a broken clock is right twice a day.* ~~All of us are destined to live our
lives between those two extremes.~~ *And every one of us — every one of us
and every one of them, we're compelled to spend our fleeting lives between those
two extremes, knowing we're never going to be right all the time and hoping we're
right more than twice a day."*

The actions of Captain Sullenberger and the oratory of President
Clinton are both amazing. Yes. They improvised. They did not however
"wing it." They did not panic. Their remarkable performances were the
result of years of experiences that culminated in making just the right
choices at just the right time.

> **Strong leadership
> requires focus**
> because...if you don't
> know where you're going
> you can't possibly expect
> people to follow you
> there.

The kind of improvisation Sully performed
on that cold January afternoon or Bill Clinton
showcased at the Democratic Convention is the
kind of improvisation this book invites you to
master as well. We do not wing it on stage and
it would be irresponsible for you to wing it in
something as important as your company and your relationships.

Instead of panicking however, you can be intentional in the face of the
unexpected. The planned and practiced approach is what will provide
you with the most intelligent options in the moment, when you too are
required to lead with calm, intelligence, and integrity. You can ride the
wave of the unexpected in a relaxed, composed manner.

Embrace BHAGs

Finally, I invite you to embrace the BHAGs. You know, those Big, Hairy Audacious Goals Jim Collins talked about in his book *Good to Great*. Maybe you've been holding out for just the right moment. Okay. Here it is. It's now.

This book arms you with an actionable definition,

To YES, AND!
ACCEPT reality,
BUILD to the greatest potential, and
ACT at the highest level.

Improvisers know their stuff and take time to master the skills. Malcolm Gladwell, author of *Blink* and *Outliers*, although not a stage performer, knows this too. He says, "...the truth is that improv isn't random and chaotic at all... Every week they [the actors] get together for a lengthy rehearsal... Why do they practice so much? Because improv is an art form governed by a series of rules, and they want to make sure that when they're up on stage, everyone abides by those rules."[3]

It's no surprise then that individuals and companies — able to understand and apply improvisation — flourish. Did you also know that the chief executive of Twitter, Dick Costolo, started out as an improviser and still uses it today? And, Twitter was not his first or only success?

Recently, because of Twitter's success, *The New York Times* provided readers with an overview of Costolo's path from comedian to social media giant.

---

[3] Gladwell, Malcolm. 2005. *Blink: The Power of Thinking Without Thinking.* Little, Brown and Company.

> "During the early 1990s, he worked at Andersen Consulting to subsidize his comedy career. He tried to explain this thing called the World Wide Web to his bosses, but, he says, they didn't listen. So he and several co-workers started their own consulting firm...
>
> Mr. Costolo went on to help found and sell three companies. One of them, Spyonit, notified people when a website changed. (This was a decade before anyone had heard the term "real time.") People used Spyonit to monitor auctions on eBay and to see when comment threads were updated on Web forums. Another of his companies, FeedBurner, helped bloggers syndicate content. FeedBurner was sold to Google in 2007 for more than $100 million."

Not bad. Even more amazing, he attributes his success to the improv principle of "Yes, And!" The article goes on to say:

> "Mr. Costolo has come a long way, too, since his comedy club days. In Chicago, he once was a co-host for a comedy show about a fake university course called "Modern Problems in Science." The audience would decide the roles of the comedians, who then posed as professors. At one show, for example, the troupe had to prove that "ugly things fall faster than pretty things."
>
> Those nights taught Mr. Costolo a number of lessons that he now applies to running a company of 1,300 employees. He rarely uses the word "but." Instead, he says "Yes, and..." — an improv principle that allows people to discuss something without disagreeing.
>
> He also says improv taught him how to see things through to the end."[4]

---

4   Bilton, Nick. "A Master of Improv, Writing Twitter's Script." October 6, 2012. *The New York Times.* http://www.nytimes.com/2012/10/07/technology/dick-costolo-of-twitter-an-improv-master-writing-its-script.html?smid=tw-share&_r=0

The company succeeds because of his openness to new ideas. Because he takes business seriously and can laugh at himself, he seizes opportunity.

As you move throughout your day, you can do the same. Use these simple three steps to accomplish your own BHAGs:

1. Start with **"YES"** — **ACCEPT** reality — acknowledge the parameters, people, and problems you face
2. Add the **"AND"** — **BUILD** to the greatest potential — add what's needed to make action possible
3. Decide and do — **ACT** at the highest level and inspire others to do the same

Most of all, keep a smile on your face and have fun!

This book invites you to explore improvisation as a way to "unfix" your attitude. Armed with a new attitude and the skills that go along with it, you can open a bunch of doors. And I mean a bunch. Doors you never knew were there.

PLAY LIST
→ Yes, And!
→ Accept reality
→ Build to the greatest potential
→ Act at the highest level

PART ONE: ACCEPT

Start with "YES" — ACCEPT reality —
acknowledge the parameters, people, and
problems you face. This doesn't get you out
of the box, but it gets you started.

1

Accept Reality

*What a trifling difference determine[s] which shall survive, and
which shall perish!*
Charles Darwin

When my father, his sister, and my grandparents escaped
Nazi Germany and fled to Brazil, they were in survival
mode. They were fortunate to get out of Germany with
false baptismal papers and each other. The long boat trip to a new
continent allowed them to rest, eat, and be. To survive. They arrived
in Sao Paolo, Brazil, safely but with little money. My grandmother, at
least initially, wanted to keep a low profile. She wanted to live within
the family's means and not take any risks. She was a brilliant, strong
woman, but understandably frightened and shaken to the core. The
threat to their survival? Fear.

My grandfather, however, was ready to take a risk. He was ready to go
beyond survival mode and begin thriving. He had to. Unable to get
a work visa, he needed to find a way to feed his family. He rented an
expensive apartment in the best area of town.

My grandmother panicked. "Theo, we cannot afford this. We will not
even be able to buy furniture, let alone food."

"Francis, I have a plan. Please be patient."

After renting the expensive unit, my grandfather began to scrounge the city for discarded furniture. Furniture that others no longer had use for and had tossed to the curb. He brought each piece home and with careful craftsmanship restored the chair, the table, the china cabinet to its original glory. He kept this up until the apartment was entirely furnished.

And then, in his brilliance, he implemented the final stage of his plan. He held an "estate" sale. Because of the address he'd chosen, because the high rent district implied wealth, the apartment swarmed with buyers. They made enough money to come to the states and thrive.

Just imagine what would have happened if my grandfather had refused to accept their reality. Thankfully, he didn't.

> **It is not the strongest** of the species that survives, nor the most intelligent, but the one most responsive to change.

For most of us, the stakes are seldom that high but they are still significant.

Denial is delusional; rooted in the belief that whatever the moment has given you will go away if you just focus on something else.

In my workshops, I demonstrate the power of "no" this way. I ask for one volunteer to join me up front. While the others look on, I whisper to the volunteer that when we ask for a suggestion of a location, he will play the scene as if we are actually in that location. He may not use actual objects. Each object must be "created" out of thin air and "used" by the volunteer. I will tell him that I will try to ruin the scene. This doesn't take much work.

For every gesture the volunteer makes, I deny the reason for the gesture. I deny existence of the object. In fact, I deny the existence of the location. Instead of going with the volunteer to the location they create, I remain in "reality," the real room in which we are standing.

Here's an example after the audience gave us the suggestion of a beach.

Volunteer: "Beautiful day for the beach. I love the feel of sand under my feet."

MJ: "I don't feel any sand."

Volunteer: "Oh, that's because you're standing on your towel. Step off and you will."

MJ: "I don't see a towel or sand. In fact, all I see is the magenta carpet."

Volunteer: "Maybe you need some sunscreen. I brought some along with our lunch in my backpack."

MJ: "But I don't see a backpack and I certainly don't need sunscreen. We're in Breakout Room B in Building 21."

As you can see from even this short exchange, it's tedious and painful. I let it go on awhile to allow the audience to see how much work the volunteer has to do. He or she is doing all the heavy lifting by making all the suggestions. I just wait and shoot them down.

The amazing part (or maybe it's not so amazing) is that every time I get volunteers up to play a scene, they do it well. They immediately see and live in the environment. They create and use the objects. They even get protective when I start "destroying" them.

Afterward, we stop, applaud the volunteer, and talk about what happened. One of my first questions is, "Where were your sympathies?"

Response: "With the volunteer, of course. He was trying so hard. He was actually at the beach. I wanted to be there with him. He was doing all the work."

I then ask, "What did you think of me?"

Response: "You were a jerk. You ruined the scene. You weren't even trying. You wouldn't cooperate. You didn't agree to anything the volunteer said."

And they are right. All those things were true.

I ask for other comments.

"It was painful to watch. If that went on any longer I think I'd scream."

The interesting part is that the participant and much of the audience see the beach. Many go beyond the backpack and the sand. They hear the waves; they see a sandcastle or a lighthouse. The entire scene comes into view. The environment springs to life. We want to believe. These responses show just how badly we want to believe.

But after my repeated denials, the beach goes away, and so does the energy. They've just witnessed how difficult it is to "play" a scene, or work together, when one member of the team refuses to listen and build on the ideas of the others.

You've probably experienced this most directly in a meeting. The meetings go on forever because we each put up one roadblock after another. We spend precious time shooting down brave teammates daring to offer ideas.

We deny in a variety of ways. Here are just a few examples.

- We don't listen. More recently in our culture, we don't even pretend to listen. We burrow into our iPads and smartphones. We surf the Web. We text or answer emails. In our defense, many speakers don't give us much reason to listen.
- We criticize every idea. We don't even give the idea room to breathe before we're saying things like, "Before every show possibly afford that? We tried that three years ago and it was a huge mistake."

- We sit quietly, so quietly that we become the focus of the meeting. We say we're just listening, but by not adding at all to the conversation, others begin to speculate. "She doesn't like the idea. She's apathetic. She doesn't understand what we're talking about. She's bored. She must be mad at someone in the room."
- We hear the idea and seize on it. We take it over, make it our own, and bully the other team members into moving forward in a particular way. We like the power. We demand our way. We exclude other options.
- We're bored, and our laptop battery is low. We didn't get enough sleep the night before or we're fighting a hangover. Perhaps we've been to too many meetings. Whatever the reason, we derail the meeting. We interrupt the flow of conversation with jokes at the expense of another teammate. Our distractions eliminate any possibility of accomplishment.

It doesn't take long for participants to see themselves as the one who keeps us from enjoying the "beach." And not just the beach: each other, our ideas, our resources. They get a glimpse of how others perceive them when they are the ones blocking productivity and innovation.

Saying no comes easily to most of us. We do it out of fear, impatience, and bias. We think:

- If I say yes, I have no idea where this might take us.
- I'm in charge and I can't afford to be wrong, so I'm going to stick with what I know.
- I didn't think of the great idea so I sure don't want anyone else getting the credit.
- I don't like this person, so I'm pretty sure I won't like any of his or her ideas.
- It'll take too long to figure out a new way, and the research would be too expensive.

Let's face it, we don't like to look bad or be wrong. Playing it safe feels like it might help protect us from both of those.

Leave Your But Behind

How many times today have you said "No" to another person? Maybe you say the word "But" instead. Either way, you probably don't think you say it very often. Most of us aren't aware of how often we say "No." Saying "No" is a lot like slamming doors. We slam shut opportunities with customers. We lock out ideas. We close down communication. We turn our backs on the very people who can help us. We start leading with our "But" so to speak. After awhile, all the slamming starts to weaken the hinges and irritate the neighbors.

← NO looks like this.

Improvisation helps keep the doors open, even during a storm. In fact, it's the best protection in all kinds of weather. But we still have to suit up and get out there.

Playing it safe doesn't work. When you first got into business, you had a taste for adventure. It was thrilling to try new things. But, you got knocked around some, lost some money, hired the wrong person and chased the wrong customers. You got cautious and tired. Time and experience now tempts you to play it safe. Or maybe you're still gunning for the adventure and willing to take the risk, while the people around you have retreated.

The tools of improvisation move you out of your comfort zone to see the world (your business, your clients, your loved ones, your friends) in a new way. It encourages you to reverse this resistance to risk and change, and that's contagious, quickly spreading to the rest of your team.

PLAY LIST
→ Tell the truth
→ Allow for mistakes
→ Make each other look great

2

Accept Yourself

*Anything I've ever done that ultimately was
worthwhile initially scared me to death.*
Betty Bender

My first year teaching high school in Michigan taught me a huge lesson about myself. The head of the English department asked me to teach a college prep World Literature class. Unfortunately, I never formally studied World Literature. Unconcerned over what I thought was a major gap, he assigned me the class anyway.

The nine smartest kids in the school — and only those nine – signed up. They entered the room on the first day of class and I instantly knew I would be the most challenged person in the class.[5]

To manage my angst, I over prepared. I spent hours reading, researching and memorizing. Then, using the podium as protection, I commenced my lecture. I talked fast, knowing high-performing students capture every syllable in their notes on the way to the coveted "A." My rate of speech allowed no time for questions. Answering questions surely would expose my ignorance. I told them the "right" answers. They

> **Etymology of the *worry*:** *"The ancestor of our word, Old English wyrgan, meant "to strangle." Its Middle English descendant, worien, kept this sense and developed the new sense "to grasp by the throat with the teeth and lacerate" or "to kill or injure by biting and shaking."[5] Basically, when you're worrying, you're choking.*

---

[5]   Worry. *The Free Dictionary.* http://www.thefreedictionary.com/worry

wrote them down. This worked extremely well for the first three days. The fourth day, my confidence brought my demise.

I began my lecture on the great Francis Bacon. You know the overachiever from the 1500s — the statesman, lawyer, philosopher, writer, and speaker. He even conducted experiments on how to freeze chicken. John W. Cousins describes his intellect as "one of the most powerful and searching ever possessed by man, and his developments of the inductive philosophy revolutionized the future thought of the human race."[6] He was, and is still, a big deal.

I started my lecture and erroneously referred to him as "Jeffrey" Bacon. I panicked.

Tim, one of the nine braniacs, raised his hand. With only 10 of us in the room, I couldn't pretend I didn't see it. I hesitated and tried to act annoyed to buy some time. It didn't work. His arm, a flag to my ignorance, continued to wave. I had to acknowledge him.

"Yes, Tim."

"Don't you mean Francis Bacon?" His face earnest, he was looking to me to provide wisdom and direction.

Then it started. "On no, I mean Jeffrey Bacon. Everyone knows about Francis Bacon but it was his brother Jeffrey that made many of the contributions that we savor today. In fact, the Bacon brothers brought us the scientific, legal, and philosophical thinking that has changed our world dramatically. Francis has received much of the notoriety, but Jeffrey…"

I continued at a furious clip, as if anxious to fill every moment with Bacon brothers' trivia that eluded historians for years. When they tried to work out a hand cramp, I paused only briefly. The upcoming test

---

[6]   Cousins, John W. 1910. *A Short Biographical Dictionary of English Literature*. London, J.M. Dent & Co.

required they capture every word in their notes. I hurried on until the bell rang. They left. I collapsed.

Initially, I reveled in my brilliance. Then, I recognized the repercussions. I lied to the nine smartest kids in the school. That was bad. Worse yet, it was a Christian school. Even worse, I knew they'd be back the next day.

Doomed, I spent a long night waiting for the principal to call. He didn't. In the morning, the class re-entered the scene of the crime, eager to "learn" more. I had a choice, continue to lie or come clean.

I stepped out from behind the podium. Exposed, I pulled out the awkward little desk chair, and sat down. They were uncomfortable, and so was I.

"There is no Jeffrey Bacon." Gasps.

"But you lectured yesterday all about the Bacon brothers."

"I know. I'm sorry. I panicked." Pause. "When Tim attempted to correct me, I didn't know what to do. As the teacher, I thought I'm supposed to know everything and I don't. Clearly. When I said the wrong name I didn't have the guts to tell you I was wrong."

I don't like making mistakes. I don't like rejection. I like to be right. But that actually turned out to be one of the better moments of my teaching career. By admitting that I was fallible — by being honest —I became the better leader. By talking together about what I did and why I did it, we built relationships. We learned from each other instead of my just spewing stuff I read the night before. Now there was room to make mistakes. We replaced hierarchy with collaboration.

Stop Saving Your Face

In my workshops, I ask people, "Are you willing to look foolish?" If they hesitate, the next question I ask is, "What's the worst that can possibly happen, if you do look foolish?" For some, just

> "A product is the extension of a human soul."
> *Walter S. Taylor*

feeling foolish may be the worst. If getting an A in a class was your primary goal, this will be a hurdle. Believing there is one only right answer makes this even harder.

A willingness to look foolish allows for the possibility that there is more than one right answer — perhaps no answer at all. If you can read a profit/loss statement, this is the last thing you want to hear. You want to know that your next move will either reduce expenses or increase revenue. It's that simple.

Except it's not that simple. The minute people become part of the equation, the questions and answers get complex. People are messy. And that's good. The complexity provides the challenge that gets us up in the morning. The solutions to those challenges bring innovation and ultimately satisfaction — think of Zappos, Google, and Disneyland®.

To get to their "solution" however required a level of vulnerability. If any one of those founders decided it was more important to "save face" than innovate, we would not be watching fireworks in the Magic Kingdom. (I fully recognize there might be an up side to this, if you've ever eaten a corn dog with Mickey Mouse ears on your head and a screaming two-year-old in your arms.)

Just remember, we all want others to believe we are doing great. If we look, past the starched shirts or dreadlocks, everyone else is probably just as terrified.

PLAY LIST
→ Scare yourself a little
→ Recall your "Bacon" story
→ Leave your but behind

3

Yes, And!

To Yes, And! is to accept reality, build to the
greatest potential, and act at the highest level.

D id you ever notice that if something is really funny, no one
had to tell you? No one had to say, "My, that's really funny."
If it's funny, you know it. The reaction is immediate. It's
truthful. When people try to be funny, it can be excruciating. When
they try to explain it, it's even worse.

When something's funny, people laugh. And, they laugh at the same
time. They lock eyes and start nodding. They agree. They mirror each
other.

You've heard, "There's nothing funnier than the truth." You laugh
when you're surprised and there is nothing more surprising than
someone telling the unadulterated truth. You observed it but didn't dare
say it. They say it. You gasp and laugh at the same time.

That's Yes, And! — the foundation of
improvisation. To Yes, And! is to accept reality.
That's where we started. Once we accept, we
can build.

Building looks something like the diagram here.
It starts with Yes. If you stop there, however,

you'll notice you're still in the box. You stopped. It's better than No, but not by much.

Yes is a start. You're listening. You at least heard what the other person said. This also means you might even be open to hearing more.

Yes

In my workshops, I demonstrate Yes in this way. I tell the volunteer that no matter what he or she says, I will agree but I will stop there. I will just say Yes. We then get a location from the audience and begin the scene. For example:

Audience Suggestion: Bus Station

Volunteer: "From the schedule board, it looks like our bus is going to be late."

MJ: "Yup."

Volunteer: "I'll put our stuff in a locker so we don't have to carry it around."

MJ: "Okay."

Volunteer: "Will you hold the key so it doesn't get lost?"

MJ: "Sure."

Volunteer: "I'm hungry. Let's get something to eat."

MJ: "Okay."

The scene is boring. There's little energy or forward movement. The volunteer is doing all the work. The audience sees the objects we create but quickly loses interest. I become superfluous.

We all know plenty of people who say "Yes." They want to be liked. They don't want to take sides. They believe being agreeable is a positive trait. The problem is they won't commit to anything. We can't count on them, but we also can't count them out because we don't know where they stand.

Yes, And!

Next, I demonstrate Yes, And! Again, we ask for a location. My whispered instructions to the volunteer are simple. Whatever one of us initiates in the scene, the other person's responsibility is to agree and build on that idea. We won't deny. We won't block any suggestion. We also don't stop at "Yes." Each suggestion must be met with Yes, And!

Audience Suggestion: A garage

Volunteer: "This is a huge garage."

MJ: "Biggest garage on the street."

Volunteer: "But there's no car."

MJ: "I couldn't afford the car after I bought the garage."

Volunteer: "Too bad. It's perfect for a car."

MJ: "Totally agree. I was wondering if you'd mind if I borrowed your car."

Volunteer: "I don't mind. Here are the keys." (Digs them out of his pocket.)

MJ: "Unbelievable. I never thought you'd let me drive your Aston Martin."

Volunteer: "Oh sure. What's mine is yours."

MJ: "Great. Let me get Rufus, my Great Dane. He's nuts about British cars."

There are lots of ways you can go with this scene. But what you see immediately is there is a much greater sense of play. The energy is always higher in this last scene. There is more laughter. The scenes are more innovative.

> **"Improvisation is** intuition in action."
> *Stephen Nachmanovitch*

When we ask the audience what they thought of this scene, they always love it. They love it for the reasons above and they love it because they become fully present in the scene. When I ask why it worked, their answers include, "Because you were both playing. Because you built the scene together. You were in the same place."

When I ask what objects they saw they immediately respond: "The garage. The car. The leather seats. The huge dog." They even end up shouting out things we didn't create...the shovel, the toolbox, a bunch of hoses. It's amazing how real the scenario becomes. If two or more people see and agree on something, it's there.

> **"Exercises used by actors** to develop their skill can be adopted by business as a means to experience and enhance individual and organizational capacity to be innovative and responsive."
> *T&D Magazine*

Yes, And! allows you to think much more broadly. It allows you to consider options you may not even know exist. Yes, And! requires careful listening. It encourages thoughtful consideration. It celebrates collaborative innovation. It moves us to work together and actually do something. Yes, And! creates an atmosphere where ideas are welcome and people are respected.

It allows everyone to be a part of the play, the solution, and energy. Using Yes, And! requires the participants to build on one another's ideas in order to develop the idea to its fullest.

With Yes, And!, the vision comes alive. If you want to reach your goals, invent a new product, solve a world problem, create harmony and get others to see it with you. Engage their senses. That's all it takes. You can't inspire them if they can't experience it with you.

The only real way to lose is to say "No." It's true, ideas are a dime a dozen. But there is only one of each individual. The unique perspective of each person is of huge value to all of us. When you say No, people shut down, even if they appear to acquiesce. The unfortunate result is that the next time they have an idea they won't come to you. They will keep their brilliant ideas to themselves.

Remaining open and agreeable to others' ideas is the best way to discover innovative solutions and retain relationships. Remember, each unique individual can contribute unique solutions. If we lose one member of the conversation, we lose all those solutions.

Nonverbal Behavior

Our words get drowned out by what we say with our bodies, facial expressions, and tone. It's not just speaking the words Yes, And! It's our actions and posture. It's an eye roll or a smirk. It's a dismissal as you reach for your phone. It's anything that shuts another person down. The following visuals help remind us of this.

PoRIFS

When another person comes to you and expresses an idea, attitude, or perception and you say "NO" either with your words or nonverbal behavior, IT'S LIKE TURNING YOUR BACK ON HIM OR HER. If this person starts to take action and you shut him or her down, squelch the enthusiasm, or cause doubt, it's the same. It's a big, loud "NO."

YES, BUT...isn't much better. We might feel better about it. "Hey, at least I was open to the idea." Still, we've shut down the communication. It just took us a little longer to do it.

"YES, OR..." is little better still. When another person comes to you and expresses an idea, attitude, perception, and you say, YES, you are at least continuing the conversation... for a little while. But, as you can see from the illustration, the two of you are facing different directions

And then there's YES, AND! And with that comes energy, enthusiasm, and momentum. Ideally, everyone is thrilled to be going in the same direction. You're celebrating, having fun, laughing, and can't wait to get moving on whatever it is.

Even if you're not quite ready to throw a party, you'll notice that, at least now, you are all facing in the same direction. You have the opportunity to see the world as those around you see it. To climb into their skin. Walk a mile in their shoes. See through the lenses of their glasses.

Whatever way you want to say it, you've changed your perspective.

And, of course, this gets us to collaboration doesn't it? Cooperating, working together...allowing for, as they say, a meeting of the minds. YES, AND! Good stuff.

Common Questions About Yes, And!

1. Does Yes, And! mean we can never disagree?

No. We do not need to Yes, And! people who are dishonest, testing us, or manipulating us. Agreement is rooted in the truth.

2. Isn't Yes, And! time consuming?

Yes, And! does take time. Whether or not it's more time is debatable. One way or another you're going to put time in. By choosing to put the time in at the beginning, you will save time in the long run.

> **"Used properly, [the games]** are a learning system which can reach the intuitive power of the individual and release genius."
> *Viola Spolin*

What takes the real time is dealing with all the conflict from saying, No, Yes Or, and Yes But. And the cost of missing out on ideas and the contribution of the team is incalculable.

Frankly, most of the time, the initial conversation doesn't take long. In addition, you've established rapport. People feel heard and the environment for collaboration is ripe.

Having the initial conversation opens the door. If you don't have time to explore the idea fully now, set a time when you can get together next. At that point, the idea may have fizzled. If not, perhaps the idea is more fully developed. Either way, you win. You have another person who knows you'll listen. They'll be more willing to return with ideas. This is how positive change starts.

It's also possible that Yes, And! may save you the very time you don't think you have. Perhaps it's a solution to the same inefficiency that is swallowing up your time every day.

3. What if someone suggests a bad idea?

I have several responses to this question.

- Who gets to say it's a bad idea? You? Remember Viola Spolin's comment, "A fixed attitude is a closed door." Perhaps you need to see things in a new way. By labeling an idea as bad, you shut out possibilities.
- Your response may be more about tensions in power or status. This is the quickest way to "pull rank." If you're not careful, you sound condescending.
- The suggestion may be a sign that you haven't established clear parameters. Others may not understand the constraints relevant to the issue. In this situation, you've wasted their time by not being clear to begin with.

Decide what's most important to you and Yes, And! that. Examples of the priority include:

- The relationship
- Time
- Quality
- Innovation
- Experimentation
- Learning

4. What if someone suggests something we tried before and it didn't work?

The answer to this question is similar to #3 with a few differences. Ask yourself:

- Have I communicated past history, experiences, and discoveries?
- Have I clarified parameters? Is it possible that attempts that didn't work before might work now? Might there be new opportunities? For example:
  - Are new materials available?
  - Could we attempt a different methodology?
  - Does this expose a blind spot?
  - Were there gaps in understanding?
  - Are they seeing the "problem" in a new way?
  - Is there more than one right answer?

5. What if I Yes, And! and others don't Yes, And! back?

Yes, And! can be lonely. You can find yourself accepting a reality others don't see or don't want to see.

Additionally, the truth is that the moment you Yes, And! one thing you are, inadvertently, saying "No" to another. Yes, And! quickly highlights our priorities.

- If the relationship is more important, I am excluding other things that may take that same time. For example, I'll spend time over a nice dinner but not finish that report.
- If I choose to save money on a process, I may not get the quality I want.
- If I buy this house, I won't be living in another one.

6. How can we use Yes, And! in the evaluation phase of a project without dampening the enthusiasm of the team?

Improvisers say there are no right or wrong answers. In business however, we are quick to label decisions right or wrong. Careers soar and fail for this reason.

The enthusiasm of the team, engaging all voices, is certainly the intent of introducing this approach into the culture. Too often employees are not engaged at all levels because of a hierarchical approach to decision-making. Policies and processes can undermine ownership as well. So, recognizing the importance of engaging the team and maintaining enthusiasm is critical.

The tools of improvisation, which you'll read more about in Part Two, are not so much linear as they are holistic. In order to help us understand and use them I've broken them out into the six stages or tools. But the communication process is fluid and organic. This means we will experience them applied simultaneously.

Improvisation provides an integrated, interactive approach to sustainable culture change.

There certainly is an evaluative component with each tool. This approach does not rule out critical thinking nor can it. The idea however of listening more to each other, building on the ideas of others, respecting each other by staying in the moment, is the real value improvisation can bring to the workplace and our personal lives. By heightening relationships, we strengthen sustainable business practices by nurturing — through significant resource — human capital. By "Yes, And!-ing" at each stage of the process, we "Yes, And!" the need for data as much as we "Yes, And!" the need for hearing the idea.

As a business owner myself, I certainly understand the impact of "right and wrong answers." When we label contributions as "wrong" answers, we shut down innovation. Competitive business practices require we take risks and strive for innovative solutions. That

Ask yourself: What holds me back from building on the ideas of others?

may mean "committing" more quickly because of the value of failing early and often. If failure is seen as a positive contribution, we are more likely to learn from the experience. If we fear failure, we hide our mistakes, reduce communication, and our tentative approach results in missed opportunity.

PLAY LIST
→ Listen more to avoid "Yes Or..."
→ Stop yourself from "Yes But..."
→ Offer up "Yes, And!" whenever you can

PART TWO: BUILD

BUILD to the greatest potential —
add what's needed to make action possible by:
Finding your focus
Staying in the moment
Attending to who/what/where
Allowing for give and take
Taking steps to commit

Yes, And! Focus

A person who is gifted sees the essential point and
leaves the rest as surplus.
Thomas Carlyle

Roadkill. You want to avoid it. But isn't it surprising how often you hit it? You try to look away, but you can't. It's horrific, puzzling, even surprising. It's a distraction. It slows you down and can take you off course. In the worst of cases, the loss of focus can cause another accident.

Glenn, the instructor in my motorcycle safety course, explained the danger of distraction this way, "Whatever you look at, that's where you'll end up," he said. "So if you want to come out of that mountain curve safely, look to the end of the curve, not the beginning. And for sure don't look at the guardrail halfway through the curve." The crazy part of riding a motorcycle, beyond the obvious, is that the safest way to ride is to look where you want to go, not to where you are.

Riding a motorcycle taught me lots of amazing lessons like that. It also taught me about frostbite, how to nurse an oversized hematoma, and how to pick myself up out of a flowerbed.

Glenn's little speech, however, kept me alive. Riding a motorcycle requires a higher level of focused alertness than most activities. I had to ignore the itch on my nose, the ache in my butt, even the gas level in the tank.

Focus keeps you alive on the freeway, wins you a bear at a carnival, and forces you to stop perseverating on the stain on your shirt. It's that ability to block out all the extraneous information and zero in on one thing. Sometimes it's the most important thing. Sometimes it's irrelevant. Some forms of mental illness come from over focusing — like obsessive-compulsive disorder. Perseveration on one task or bit of information pushes out all other information.

You can harness the power of focus to get where you're going much more efficiently. Knowing what to focus on can positively affect your business. It can help you identify key resources, provide clarity for decision-making, and determine long-term strategy. Focus unifies teams, increases energy, and heightens morale. Focus is the reason you frame the mission of your company in your entryway. Focus keeps us lean.

Lack of Focus

We all know what causes a lack of focus. We're overloaded with information. Our senses are over stimulated. We have access to too much information — much of what we don't need. We receive mixed messages. It's unclear what's expected of us. We're required to act quickly but provide elaborate performance plans. We're measured on everything and recognized for little.

We arrive home exhausted with work spilling out of our computer case. We feed the dog, the kids, and ourselves without knowing what we ate. We go to bed with the presentation unfinished and the wet load of laundry still in the washer. We're smart enough to know the impact — loss of productivity, profit, morale, motivation, and innovation — but stretched too thin to do anything about it. We spend one more day doing less with more.

Defining Focus

- The focus, or a focal point, is the center of an activity, attraction, or attention. For example, the focus of the meeting was customer service.
- Whatever commands and directs our attention and we then emphasize is the focus or the point of concentration.

Once we find our focus, we are free to innovate. Once we know where we're going, we can play with how we get there. The hard part is finding the focus. Harder still is maintaining it.

Tape Ball

Before every show at *The Second City* we warmed up with a tape ball. Instead of reviewing running orders, we went on stage with a raggedy oval shaped "ball" made out of duct tape. We would hit the ball to each other, a hit not a catch, to try to get to 50 without the ball touching the floor. At first it was difficult. Some, to show off, would hit it too hard. Some were tentative and would hit it too soft. Others weren't paying attention and missed the ball altogether.

When I first joined the cast and they invited me on stage, I thought this was a ridiculous way to spend the moments we had before the show. I wanted to talk about scenes or review the nuances of a character I created or, at the very least, go to the bathroom one more time. But, understanding the importance of ensemble and recognizing my fellow actors were all bigger than me and could hurt me if they liked, I stepped out on stage. At first, I was distracted, thinking about what I had in the refrigerator to eat after the show or wondering if I would remember the running order in the flurry of scenes, or glancing to see if the director was in the theater and — if he was —was he watching me.

After a few minutes, however, I found myself completely immersed in the game. All I could look at and think about was that dumb tape ball. And, of course, that was exactly the point. By the time we went backstage, we were laughing and relaxed. Our focus became the moment and the task at hand. The stress and distractions were gone. The laughing brought us together as a cast, allowing us to connect on stage. Our body language was different because of it, we listened better because of it, we found solutions to scenes we wouldn't have because of it, and we were funnier.

> **Ask yourself:** What keeps me from seeing the essential point?

The simple act of focusing made us more efficient and productive. We wouldn't have used those words, but that's exactly what it did. That's exactly what it can do for you as well.

Multitasking

Culturally, we have this goofy idea that we can do more than one thing at a time. We call it multitasking and we say the word with a sense of bravado. We act as if we're so important we must do more than one thing at a time.

Research does show that we can do two or more things at the same time. We just do them poorly. The other option is to do one thing at a time and do it well. It's a choice.

I suppose you could be an anomaly. Perhaps you can speak coherently, make meaningful decisions even as you play Spider Solitaire, and write your progress reports, but most of us can't.

This of course does not apply to all tasks equally. You can mow the lawn and chew gum at the same time. Neither activity is dependent on a real connection with another person, so it doesn't much matter if the quality slips…unless you own a landscaping business and you're prone to choking.

The point to remember is that when the moment involves another person, dividing our attention ends up dividing our results. Interestingly, we seldom multitask with the people we really value in our lives: a lover, a client, a guest — unless we take them for granted. One of the most loving things you can do for another person is to give them your full attention.

It's when we split our attention that we diffuse our energies and our resources. We do half a job and do it poorly.

Not Trusting Yourself

Seeking too much approval hurts focus, too. People often ask me after a performance if I heard the laughter. Typically I don't, at least on a conscious level. Obviously, it registers enough for me to maintain timing during a performance, but I don't play to the laughter. And I shouldn't. If I do, I find myself expecting it, waiting for it. The performance then becomes inauthentic because I fail to stay true to the character or the scene.

If you're a writer, you can't write to win a prize or even sell a book. You write because you have something to say, or a unique way to say it.

Seeking approval, aiming for a prize or waiting for applause pulls me out of the moment. My attention when performing requires that I focus singularly on the needs of my character. I must be wholly in the moment. I have to be wildly awake to the actions and words of the other characters, too.

My focus as a business owner likewise needs to be squarely on my customer. If I'm listening just to make a sale, it becomes obvious. If I'm "networking" because my motivation is purely my own well-being, people can tell. We know when people are using us, and we don't like it.

When I listen to my customers, it's just the same as when I'm listening on stage. I focus singularly on their needs. I watch body language. I listen for tone. I pay attention to the environment. I stay focused on the reason we're meeting.

My attention needs to be on them rather than myself. That means, like the laughter and applause, I'm not focused on their approval. I'm focused on their need, their objective, and how I can meet that.

Hunger and Exhaustion

Eat a good breakfast. Get plenty of rest. Exercise. You've heard this all your life. You still don't always do it, do you? I can't preach on this. I'm not exactly a poster child for work/life balance either.

I do notice however that when I do the things I'm supposed to (eat right, sleep, and exercise) I find and maintain focus much more easily.

Just Relax

The last thing you want to hear before you deliver a presentation is "just relax." It does help though. The unfortunate part is that as soon as you try to relax, you can't. "Trying" puts the focus on ourselves rather than the thing we're after. "Trying" makes us tighten up and stresses us out.

Relaxing is paramount though. People mirror what they see in others. During a show, if I'm uptight, my fellow players become uptight. If I appear nervous on stage, the audience gets nervous for me. If I am uncomfortable in a meeting with a client, the client will be uncomfortable too.

In one of my exercises, I ask participants to clap as part of a pattern. They all do, without thinking and without any problems. A few minutes later, after changing the rules and intentionally raising the stress level, I ask them to perform a similar action. Surprisingly, most of them can no longer clap. I'm not exaggerating. They just can't put their hands together. They are so worried about doing it wrong that they seize up.

It always amazes me that it takes just minutes to reduce their ability to perform to the lowest level. Never underestimate the power of stress to drastically change even the best business model.

The greatest thing we can do to get people to perform at their best is to create an environment free of stress, or at least to reduce the strain. True, stress can increase adrenaline and improve performance, but it has to be the right kind and the right amount. We do our best work when our shoulders are down and our lungs are breathing.

You can help reduce the stress by paying attention to body language — your fellows' and your own. Eye contact allows others to see us as secure and honest (unless of course you're staring). Nonverbal

> **Ask yourself:**
> What signals am I sending through my body language?

signals like nodding let others know we are paying attention. Leaning toward others when they speak and smiling invites information and creates a connection. This is all to say that, once you know who you are, you can freely take your eyes off yourself and focus on the other person.

Okay, once you start focusing on the other person, then what? It's simple. Before you perform, present to an audience, sell your widget, or provide a performance review, ask yourself this question: "What is the **one thing** this person, this group, needs to know and why?" Note the question is not "What do you want to say and why?" It's not about you. This is disconcerting I know.

Your job is to determine what this other person, these people, must to know, do, and believe to fulfill their needs. You are there for them. You have their best interest in mind. Your job is to wrap the message in the most memorable way possible. Entertain them. Surprise them. Scare them. Inform them. Whatever. Just get them there.

Finding a way to get your audience to pay attention to your message isn't easy because you are fascinated by what you want to say and they are fascinated by themselves.

Like you, your clients prefer to think, hear, sing, play, and work at things that matter to them.

Your ability to play to their unique needs and interests makes all the difference. We all pay closest attention to messages that affect our values, beliefs, and well-being. If it matters to them, it had better matter to you. This becomes especially important when delivering the difficult messages.

> **"The secret** of being tiresome is to tell everything." *Voltaire*

When I taught high school, before I walked into a new class at the beginning of the semester, I would spend time trying to find out what kids were saying about me. What was the buzz about the class? I wanted to know everything. It wasn't always easy to hear, but it did mean I was aware of the assumptions and myths. I recognized that students already had their ideas about who I was. Without ever meeting me, some even made up their minds about whether or not they liked me!

Taking time to understand the audience also has proved helpful in starting my business and connecting with clients. Knowing the assumptions and expectations allows you to be prepared for misgivings and misinformation. Knowing their preconceived notions allows you to address those directly and create an experience that more accurately represents who you are and what your company does.

What happens when you find the focus and commit to it 100 percent? That's a good thing. Yes. Unless you're focusing on the wrong thing... like I did once halfway through my first show at *The Second City*.

Falling Off the Stage

Raised in a Jewish home, a convert to a Protestant denomination, and dressed to play a Dominican nun, I grabbed my chair, ran out from backstage, and hurtled through the blackness of the 350-seat cabaret theater. Instead of finding my spike mark, I sailed into the audience and landed squarely on my right butt cheek, just shy of the first row of tables full of martinis and oversized pretzels. I had no choice but to be in the moment. Still clutching my chair, I saw the stage lights snap to full. Blinded now as well, I looked at the stage and saw my fellow actors in place, ready to begin the scene. I was supposed to be on stage with them. In fact, I was supposed to be stage right, sitting in a chair, facing the audience, and doing imaginary needlework. Instead, I was flat on my back on the floor, four and a half feet down from the lip of the stage — the wooden stage chair now entombed in my black nun's habit.

I rolled on my face. Once on my knees I did my best not to look at the audience. I vaguely remember a communal sucking sound. Somehow, I stood, scrambled to the steps, and, still grasping my prop chair, stepped squarely on my habit. Instantly I slammed chin first onto the steps. It wasn't my background, my conversion, or my dress that made this a religious moment. It was the sheer terror of facing the audience, my fellow players, and my producer.

My first performance at *The Second City* in Detroit, in *Generation X Files*, was in the scene "Granny's Records." The setting was the upstairs of a Catholic church at the funeral of an older nun. Two nuns and a priest play the deceased's favorite music during the somber service. The music begins and, to their horror, the lyrics are obscene. As soon as they realize what the next rhyme will be, they reach to stop the music before the words escape from the loudspeaker. Unfortunately, for them, it's a bit too late each time, and the implication is clear to the audience. As they rummage through her collection, each song is bawdier than the next.

For the scene to surprise and amuse the audience, I had to have thick gray prescription prop glasses, a long black habit, a headpiece, and my prop chair in place in the 30 seconds of lights-out between scenes. Backstage, sightless and soundless, each of us had just seconds to change costumes. We then raced onstage in the dark to the assigned spike mark, the designated spot to begin the scene. (The marks are pieces of glow tape on the stage that, like lights on a runway, help the actors land safely on their places in the dark.

The stage manager, though a kind and gentle person, was unfortunately not detail-oriented. Apparently, earlier that afternoon, he painted the stage but hadn't had a chance to replace all the tape. Let me just say that to leave off some spike marks randomly is to encourage the kind of horror we normally witness on the evening news: skidding into an icy bay in New England, careening into treetops, or, in my case at *The Second City*, plummeting past a squealing patron while clutching a chair.

Since I couldn't find my mark, I lost my way. Despite the humiliation, the comfort of the moment was that I wasn't alone. My fellow players were as much a part of that moment as I was. What happened to one happened to all. They could not and did not ignore what happened, and they did their best to help me find my way back into the scene.

I checked my chin to ensure it wasn't dislocated, scrambled up the steps, plopped my chair stage right, and sat down. I could feel the tilted wig on my head and struggled to see through my thick prop lenses. Margaret, also playing a nun, and Eric, in his priestly garment, came over to me immediately. I remember Margaret saying, "Sister Doreen, it appears you're late again. Perhaps you're not feeling well." I didn't answer. I couldn't. I was too busy trying to see, remember my first line, and manage my emotions — perilously close to tears or hysterics.

I centered myself by taking my imaginary needlepoint out of my imaginary sewing bag, re-examining the stitch diagram, and resuming work on the imaginary Somerset bouquet pillow. The two of them, spastic from swallowed laughter, stood with their backs to the audience, creating a wall of black in front of me. I looked up sheepishly. I worried they would assign the rookie performer's enthusiastic clumsiness as ruining the show.

They didn't. Although we found more things funnier than usual during this particular performance, we played it without missing a beat. We stayed in the moment and we stayed together.

What did the audience see? A crazy nun flying off the stage, slapping her chin on the steps as she scrambled up to the stage, two other nuns shaking their heads at her antics — and ultimately the sketch they came to see. From our performance, you would have no idea that the airborne nun was not a planned part of the entertainment.

Hit the Ball

If you play a sport, try this. Stop paying attention to your form. Stop paying attention to your technique. Stop worrying about whether your opponent is better than you or worse. Stop blaming your equipment when you miss the ball.

Next time you play, tell yourself one simple thing, and do not let your attention waver. Here it is: Focus on the ball and hit it. That's it.

When I joined *The Second City*, the director handed me a reading list. One of the books was *The Art of Playing Tennis*. Now, I'm no athlete; most improvisers are not. We're cave people. On sunny days, you find us huddled in the dark, the dank

> **"Sometimes it is more important** to discover what one cannot do, than what one can do." *Lin Yutang*

smell of cigarettes and beer wafting up from the carpet. We chose the stage because we were afraid of the ball and hated physical education. My natural assumption then was that this was a book on improvisation cleverly disguised as a book on tennis. Wrong. Halfway through, I realized it actually was a book on tennis. How odd. The premise: watch the ball; hit the ball. Simplify the task. Practice the skill. Master the game.

It's important to my discovery that you know a bit about my history with the sport. About five years earlier, I had the misfortune of finding myself on a tennis court with someone who could play. I'm not sure why she agreed, but it took me only three hits to lose three balls. This came of course after numerous times of missing the ball. My friend then motioned to me to meet her at the net. Innately a kind and good person, she also was honest. She leaned in and whispered, "This game is over, and we should never play tennis again."

Years later at *The Second City*, I read the book on tennis. I understood the premise, find your focus and your body will know what to do. From performing, I knew the importance of focus. To see if this theory worked off the stage, I thought the first best way to test it would be on the tennis court. I called on my friend. Fortunately, we were still friends and she agreed to my little experiment.

We stepped onto the court. She hit the ball and, to the amazement of us both, so did I. I hit it again. And again. I hit the ball enough times in the right way to win one game. I still was no match for her skill but I certainly improved. The trick: watch the ball and hit the ball. I let go of my fear of the ball and my concern over looking foolish. Watching the ball became more important than how I stood, held the racket, or my swing. I didn't worry about what she thought of me. I didn't fret over my outfit. I focused on the ball.

That experience profoundly changed the way I understood focus. Since then, I place a much higher value on the impact that finding and sustaining focus can have in each moment.

Each of these tools of improvisation, each of these behaviors, affects choices you make every day. Choosing to find the focus in the moment, in the conversation, in your personal life is just the beginning.

Start by making decisions and sticking to them. Determine the one thing your customer, your employee, the market, your boss needs to know and stick to it. Review Jim Collins' Hedgehog Concept in his book *Good to Great* — find your passion, know what you are best at, determine what drives your economic engine, and, at the center where those three meet, focus your energies.

Pause often. Pause to reflect, observe, laugh, learn, and sleep. Pause to just rest in the moment. The pauses don't have to be long, but they do need to be long enough to help you regain energy and see the world around you in a new way. Even if you can just breathe a bit more deeply and start again, you'll feel the difference.

Stephen Nachmanovitch in *Free Play* has a great exercise to help focus. He suggests walking around and pointing at objects and calling them the wrong name. For example, point at the door and say "scrambled eggs." It doesn't matter what you call it, just give it a different name. See the object in a new way.

It's harder than it seems. It gets harder the longer you do it. The exercise forces you to look at the same old thing differently. Refreshed, we are now open to new ways of thinking. It forces neurons to get off the couch and move. Solutions that earlier eluded you now become obvious. At the very least, you are open to considering a fresh approach.

> **Ask yourself:** What changes do I need to make to improve my focus?

Finally, focus helps you simplify. You discard anything that distracts you from the main challenge. This discipline reasserts your mission, vision, and values.

One Thing

To help me find my focus, I use one simple question: "What is the one thing my audience needs to know and why?" I ask this whether I'm writing a proposal, coaching an executive, or writing a keynote speech. I use it to guide me. It helps me throw out the stuff I don't need to say. Like you, I have a lot to say. Sometimes it's to show off, like, "Hey, I've done my homework." Sometimes it's because I'm excited. I'm passionate and just assume others will be too. Sometimes it's because I'm afraid if I'm not talking, I won't get the attention. (Translate that to "the job, the promotion, or the notoriety.") As you can see, reasons for just saying what you want to say often are lame.

Saying what your audience needs to know changes the entire equation. You now recognize that, like you, everyone else, is overwhelmed with, well, everything. Meetings, to-do lists, appointments, errands, projects, and politics are just a few of the items. The last thing any of us needs is someone talking just to hear the sound of his or her own voice.

Your audience, your customers, your employees, your boss, and your peers are overwhelmed. If you confuse them, you lose them. If you bore them, they'll try to lose you.

Your message must be simple, focused, and memorable. For examples on how to do this well, watch ads on television. They are brilliant at knowing their audience, simplifying the message, and stating only what we need to know. They've done their research and used every second masterfully.

Like the ads, get to the point. Be disciplined with your message. Be ruthless with your time and theirs. Do your homework.

If you can't say why the audience should care, you should sit down. Better yet, don't stand up in the first place. We're all busy. We need you to edit yourself and help us find our way.

Focus on the needs of those around you and you'll make an impact. Focus on your customer and you'll make a sale. Focus on your teammates and you won't work alone.

5

Yes, And! The Moment

If you have one eye on yesterday and one eye on tomorrow, you're going to be cockeyed today.

Anonymous

Professor Ken Kuiper in the spring of my freshman year of college startled us one morning by exclaiming, "We have to go outside right now. If we wait until tomorrow, it will be too late." Low on sleep and nutrition like most collegians, we lumbered to our feet.

Ken was a small man, but his energy made up for anything he lacked in physicality. He hurried us along, practically bounding out into the chilly April air. He led us to a tree, waved his right arm toward the branches, and without introduction or fanfare recited the Robert Frost poem, "Nothing Gold Can Stay."

Nature's first green is gold,
Her hardest hue to hold.
Her early leaf's a flower;
But only so an hour.
Then leaf subsides to leaf.
So Eden sank to grief,
So dawn goes down to day.
Nothing gold can stay.

Initially, we stared at him. When he noticed, he said, "Look at the tree. See the buds? Look closely at the edges of the tree. These are the first leaves. They're gold, not green. Not yet. Tomorrow they'll be green. Tomorrow is too late. Today, the first green is gold." We continued to stare but slowly melted into his moment and understood.

He did that with every class he taught until he died. Anyone who took freshman English with him had the same experience. Ken Kuiper taught me, taught us, about the urgency, the power, of the moment.

> **"Every moment is precious**, precisely because it is ephemeral and cannot be duplicated, retried, captured."
> *Stephen Nachmanovitch*

We all like to believe that we're living in the moment. The phrase is certainly popular. The reality is that in any one moment, many of us are thinking ahead to the next thing we're going to say or do. Other times we're living in the past. We're reviewing who said what at the last minute. We moan over what we wish we'd said or how we got into an argument over oatmeal. We are constantly trying to shape and control our world. Thinking ahead and looking back become second nature. In the meantime, we miss now.

Staying in the moment requires maintaining awareness of the present options and opportunities, all the time. Some of us are better at this than others. When we're good at it, the impact is significant or, in the case of one particularly talented pilot, can even seem superhuman.

In the Moment

Performing at *The Second City* is as terrifying as it is exhilarating. Directors cut, rearrange, and add scenes five minutes before the show. A prop breaks. An actor calls in sick. Not much different from what you face every day.

What amazed me is that we all knew that on stage we were in it together. We made it work. We weren't perfect. We were practical. We had a job to do and, with the pressure of hundreds of people staring up at us, we did it. We had no choice.

Of course, we had a choice, but it sure didn't feel like any other choice than to make things work would be the right choice. We often said to each other before a show, "Choose energy."

Making a choice is one of the beautiful things about performing that we should do more of in the workplace. As performers, we chose to leap into the darkness together. The immediacy of the moment essentially brought us to our senses.

Humans tend to be on better behavior when others are around. A guest in the house, a customer in the reception area, or a new employee in the department has this effect. It's when we get too comfortable, or lose perspective, that we delude ourselves into thinking that we'll skip this moment or resist it. We'll hold out for a better one. The truth is, this moment is it.

> **"Only from meeting and acting** *upon the changing* moving present can improvisation be born." *Viola Spolin*

We can leap or wait for someone to push us. From my experience, our only "salvation" is to look into the eyes of another, grasp their hand, and jump together. We can do this with confidence when we prepare for the unexpected and trust those around us.

Wake Up

Seizing the moment requires heightened sensitivity. Great improvisers are wide-awake. They notice everything — the way somebody walks, the words they use, even the sound of the air conditioner in the back room.

This may be why people with Attention Deficit Disorder typically do so well with it. They soak in the moment.

Listening

Start here. Listen to others even when they don't listen to you. It's not that they don't care. It's that they are egocentric. Just like you, like all of us.

The truth is we care about things that matter to us. If it doesn't affect us or those we love, we move on. Once you acknowledge this, everything gets a lot easier. You realize that if you're going to be heard (or be entertaining, or make the sale) you must get to know your audience more intimately than you ever imagined. You need to

> **"What we see depends** mainly on what we look for." *Sir John Lubbock*

take the opportunity, as Atticus said in *To Kill A Mockingbird*, to "climb into their skin." Once you climb in, walk around in it. See the environment through their eyes. See it for the first time, each time. Great actors do this with such care we're convinced they are that person. Don't underestimate the work that goes into this craft. It's amazing.

People — employees, clients, family members, and friends — are our greatest resource. We can't afford to look past them and take them for granted. If we do, we miss out on their contributions; we miss out on them. We need to make the most of each moment with each of them now. And it has to be just that. A real, genuine moment when you aren't doing something else.

Five Steps to Spontaneity

1. Prepare

I was attracted to improvisation in part because I did think it meant you didn't have to prepare. I was disappointed to find out that preparation is what made the improvisers so good.

I realize some improvisers will disagree with me. I'm okay with that. It's good to have different perspectives. All I know is that we spent a lot of time rehearsing. If we did not have to prepare, that would mean anyone could jump onstage and entertain us with the skill of a Fred Willard, Amy Poehler, or Martin Short.

Those people are obviously talented. They've also worked hard at their craft. They are skilled artists who have been willing to put the time in to be that good.

Their preparation allows them to stay in the moment and deal with whatever happens. We call them "witty." They can be witty because they're relaxed. Confidence comes from being ready — at least as ready as you can be — for the unexpected.

Thinking ahead about the events of the day, the people you will connect with, and the kinds of expectations others have of you will help as well. Obviously, you can't think of everything, but you can try.

It's surprising that spontaneity requires preparation. The more you practice and prepare, the more likely you are to get what's in your head and heart into the heads and hearts of others.

All your preparation for more planned and formal communication will serve as an enormous reservoir of resources for when you need them.

2. Stay in the room

An improvisational scene falls apart when it becomes about someone who is not in the scene. Or about an event in the past or a place to go in the future. The audience wants to see an interesting scene right now, in front of them. They don't want to hear that something more interesting just happened or is going to happen somewhere else. We need to give them the scene they came to see.

The same is true when you're standing in front of another person. Be with him or her. Stop thinking back to what just happened or what might happen next. You chose to go there. Now it's time to be there.

3. Stop talking

My mom always said, "If you don't have anything nice to say, don't say anything."

No offense to my mother, but I don't agree with this anymore. It's not honest or direct. It doesn't allow for constructive feedback.

It does remind us, though, to talk less. To stop trying to fill the space or ease the discomfort. Sometimes we need to be uncomfortable. We learn when we're uncomfortable. Our senses wake up when we're uncomfortable.

Try to find times to hold the moment. Despite how fast everything is moving in our world, you are allowed to slow down and think before you respond.

4. Listen some more

Keep listening. The witty repartee you admire in others requires timing. Capture the moment in an unforgettable way. Get us to see the issues, others, and ourselves in ways we've never seen before. Great listening leads to great insights.

5. Act and react

Observe how your actions affect others. Instead of making communication a task to check off your list, slow down and stay in the moment. Don't rob yourself or others of the possibilities that come with a genuine interchange.

Take time to see the expression, observe the body language, and hear the tone. Slow down. Make the connection. Remember, communication goes beyond words. Pause. Hear. Receive. Respond.

Originality

In meetings, new endeavors, or in conversations, we worry about being original. From experience, this is the quickest way to squash what makes you unique. In fact, by pressuring yourself to come up with something totally original and innovative, you get tense. You get anxious. Unfortunately, anxiety spawns banality.

This is why relaxing is so critical to spontaneity. When you relax, you are the closest to the "you" you will ever experience. You can't help being yourself when you're at ease. Since there's only one of you, by default, you will be most original when you're in this state.

Being you allows everyone else in the room to relax and be himself or herself. Want to be more innovative? Want to solve a problem? Want to secure a patent? Be yourself.

If you can't be yourself with those around you, be brave and start changing the culture. If you can't accept or change the culture, move on.

PLAY LIST
→ See the first green
→ Hold the moment
→ Choose energy
→ Wake up
→ Be yourself

6

Yes, And! Who/What/Where

You never really understand a person until you consider things from his point of view – until you climb into his skin and walk around in it.
Harper Lee

The new hire at the food processing plant was what they called a "high potential" or HiPo, which is more fun to say. Bruce was motivated, worked hard, and had the right resume for the position as supervisor of the second shift. He seemed like the perfect fit. That's why it came as a surprise when the first-shift supervisor and many team leaders started to grumble. Later, their voices got louder in written and oral complaints. Finally, the first-shift supervisor, Cheryl, threatened to quit.

The executive team heard the complaints and assumed the two would work it out. They liked Bruce's strong style and his confidence. True, productivity had risen only slightly, but they figured it was just a matter of time. Later, the numbers leveled off and even started to drop. Maybe the problem was Cheryl. Either way, they had to figure out what was going on. Despite numerous conversations, the situation did not improve. The executive team invited me in to help them get along and get back to work.

The three of us met within a week. We sat in a small conference room on the first floor above the plant. We met at the end of the first shift and beginning of the second to accommodate them both. As soon as they sat down, their folded arms and turned torsos told me volumes about their feelings for each other. I noticed something else. Cheryl was fully dressed to work the line: hairnet, white jacket and pants, no jewelry, and gloves. Bruce wore street shoes, grey pants, a watch, and an open white jacket over his starched dress shirt.

I listened to the arguments and the pledges to change behavior. We came up with an action plan and I led them through some exercises. Bruce spoke calmly and a little condescendingly about why they weren't getting along. Cheryl was more emotional and just wanted to get back to work. At the end of that first session, I took Bruce aside and asked why he wasn't wearing the proper attire for working in the plant. He said he couldn't find anything to fit him at the employee center. He appeared average in size, so I suggested he try again.

The next time we met, he said the same thing about his clothing. At the end, I told Bruce that he must come dressed appropriately for being on the floor in the plant.

When he walked into the room the third time in street shoes and slacks, I told them both that we would not meet again and they should go back to work.

Later, when I met with the president, I said I would no longer work with Bruce. Although I liked having the work, I knew they were wasting money and time on someone who was not coachable.

"If you don't fire him now, you will in the next three months," I said.

"But we hired him to be a star performer," the president said.

"Maybe so, and I can see why," I responded. "He presents well at first. The problem you're having, however, with the other supervisor, the team leaders, and the line workers is that Bruce has chosen to go high-status. Instead of becoming a

> "You get the best effort from others not by lighting a fire beneath them, but by building a fire within them."
> *Bob Nelson*

47

part of the team, a leader in the trenches willing to get his hands dirty, you've hired someone who's gunning for an office upstairs. He's above them, or so he thinks, and they feel that. His unwillingness to dress for the role communicates this. No amount of coaching will change this if he's not willing to lead from within."

They didn't fire Bruce right away. But they did a couple of months later. As they say, when people show you who they are, believe them.

Defining Who/What/Where

- Who/What/Where is continuing to anticipate, assess, and adapt to the people, the issues and the environment in the moment.
- Awareness of who you are addressing, what the issues are, and the impact of the atmosphere on the message allows you to create the best environment possible for powerful, productive, positive relationships.

The better you know your surroundings and the more aware you are of them, the more likely you are to meet the needs of those around you.

WHO   People are messy. We can't turn them on and off like a machine. We can't look at an expiration date and put them in the trash. We can't reuse/recycle them for something useful like a guardrail. This doesn't mean, unfortunately, that some haven't tried. It's just that they don't "go gently into that good night."

Whether we like it or not we have to deal with them — with all their unpredictability, irrationality, and emotion. We also get to deal with their genius — often exhibited in unpredictability, irrationality, and emotion.

Perhaps it's so difficult because we assume it should be much easier. After all, we're human. Sure seems that we would have a lot in common.

As surprised as you are that they don't see things your way, they are surprised you don't see things their way. Whether you are conscious of it or not, you adhere to a set of core values. You hold them dear. You use them to make large and even small decisions. You act on them in relationships.

So do they. The problem, at least from your perspective, is they don't share the same core values but they cherish theirs to the same degree you do yours.

Like performers on a stage, we choose to play certain roles within the company. We can choose a role that supports the other players. Or we can choose a role that serves ourselves. We can be "we" players or "I" players. Productive, collaborative, profitable teams are comprised of "we" players. Bruce was out for himself. He was looking for prestige. Bruce focused on promotion above the collected good.

> **Collaboration requires** me to stop saving my own face and start saving the faces of others.

Improvisers focus on the audience. Their product is entertainment. To pull that off requires a thriving ensemble, to make a fast, funny, and original product. In business, production requires the same kind of committed team. There's no room for prima donnas. There's no room for playing by different rules. There's no room for personal success above all else.

If that's true, others have to believe that you care about their success as much as your own. In other words, they must trust you. Without trust, they won't take a risk to create the relationships we need, and neither will our customers. Without trust in our team, we won't reveal mistakes and learn from each other. We can't enhance lean processes if we can't identify the cause of the waste. We can't improve products if we don't get feedback on what's not working.

Even the title of Stephen Covey's book, *The Speed of Trust*, shows us how important trust is to productivity. He says, "more and more, people are coming to recognize the cost of low trust and are making efforts to establish and restore trust."

He knows, and we know, that a true team shares both blame and glory. There's no room for divas or stand-up comedians. Each ensemble member takes the primary job seriously: Make each other look great!

On stage, a player who keeps score on who has the funniest line, best character, most unusual idea, loudest voice, or most applause doesn't last. Each contributor needs to have the other players in mind at all times. They ask, "How can I support the choices of the other players?" "How can I make this scene better?" "Would the scene be better without me?" Sometimes, the most generous thing a player can do is stay out of the scene. Actions speak to trust. What players do strengthens or weakens trust among team members. Actions reveal who and what they value — on stage and off.

Team members develop empathy and start acting as if they care about the rest of the team because they do.

Create this environment and watch what happens. Take idea sharing for example. When someone reacts to our idea or contribution as dumb, we feel one of two ways: rejected or angry. When someone accepts our idea, we connect that to our egos. We draw positive conclusions about ourselves and the other people on the team. You might end up thinking, "I have a decent mind," or "I like this other person because they see value in me." Or "I should buy them lunch." You contribute more. You can't wait to throw in the next idea.

Communication style changes too. Direct, open conversations replace hidden agendas. Team members worry less about trying to play it safe and more about making genuine contributions.

Don't get me wrong. It's not that they no longer care if others like them. The difference is that they no longer act at the detriment of their core values. They are willing to take a stand, have a point of view.

It isn't until you have a strong sense of who you are that you can really relate to the "whos" around you. People come into sharp focus when you are clearly in focus yourself. By defining yourself, you allow others to take a definitive place of their

> **"Trades would not take place** unless it were advantageous to the parties concerned." *Benjamin Franklin*

own. They are not you and that is now easier to see.

On stage, this creates powerful theater in a short amount of time. As soon as I understand your character — what she does for a living, her idiosyncrasies, the things that make her angry — I can easily play my character "against" those particulars. If I don't know who you are, what you're doing or where we are, we will both flounder in the land of blah and blurry.

It works just as well in the boardroom.

WHAT

Stop ignoring the elephant in the room. Elephants are big and, once aroused, very loud.

When improvisers refer to the "what," they are referring to the issue in the scene. What do these people need? What is the real reason they're together? Is it an environmental challenge? ("We're locked out of the house.") Is it a relational conflict? ("I love you but you're married to someone else.") Is it an ethical challenge? ("It's not my money but I need it more than they do.")

You get the picture. Scenes are about what ties people together, whether they like it or not. The issues may be different in the workplace (or not.) That there are issues is undeniable.

This goes beyond issues between individuals. Put lots of people together with the same core values and they create a culture. If we don't take time to understand the individuals around us, we certainly can't presume to understand the culture.

How does understanding culture lead us to the "what," the issues? Fons Trompenaars and Charles Hampden-Turner nail it in the book, *Riding the Waves of Culture*. "Every culture distinguishes itself from others by the specific solutions it chooses to certain problems that reveal themselves as dilemmas."[7]

Apparently, even what we identify as a solution, problem, or dilemma is impacted by who we are as a culture. Fair to say then we had better take the time to create a shared understanding around words like success, failure, freedom, honesty, and fairness.

> **"Individually, we are one** drop. Together, we are an ocean."
> *Ryunosuke Satoro*

What about competition vs. collaboration? Does competition improve or weaken succession planning? Won't collaboration with a "competitor" weaken market share?

Clearly, competition has its downside. We build silos. We refuse to share information. We lock out solutions. The isolation causes suspicion. We worry that if others know too much about what we're doing they will take it away from us. We worry if they know too little we won't get the recognition we deserve. We want to ensure we are irreplaceable.

It's the silos that leave our companies open to attack from outside competitors.

The more similar we are, the more we compete. Competition thrives in a monoculture. Our companies suffer the same problems as the farmers. The terminology used for genetically modified seeds is an indication. Farmers refer to certain seeds as "terminators," "repressors," and "activators" — dysfunctional players trying to stop each other at

---

7   Trompenaars, Fons and Charles Hampden-Turner, 2012. *Riding the Waves of Culture*. The Macgraw-Hill Companies, Inc.

every turn. In the process of thwarting others, they burn themselves out. They destroy themselves in their effort to compete.

Unfortunately, monocultures also produce sterile environments. Monocultures invite closeout sales. Weak leaders welcome others just like themselves. Diversity is threatening. Weak leaders choose replicas of themselves because they're used to

> **"To overcome difficulties** is to experience the full delight of existence."
> *Arthur Schopenhauer*

living with themselves. They don't have the time, will, or strength to tolerate behavior that doesn't fit their norm. If they pick people like themselves, they'll know how that person approaches the project. Their reports will respond to customers exactly as they would.

Competition isn't all bad. It just can't be a bully. It has to share space with collaboration.

Darwin's birds discovered competition wasted too much energy. They were hungry. They wanted to eat. Adapting, rather than competing, was the quickest way to a full belly and more generations of finches.

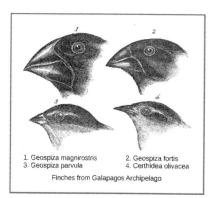

1. Geospiza magnirostris   2. Geospiza fortis
3. Geospiza parvula   4. Certhidea olivacea
Finches from Galapagos Archipelago

Their beaks tell the story. Look at the curvature, length, and shape. If every birdbrain decided they could only snack on the same, they all would disappear.

Instead, they diversified. Sounds like something your financial consultant might say to you.

Some finches chose insects. Others chose seeds. Smart. It also seems like good manners, don't you think? When they stopped competing for the same food, there was plenty for everybody. Perhaps, if we start by seeing each other as comrades rather than enemies, we'll be more likely to survive. Certainly, we'd be moving away from extinction, which is a much better direction.

Janine M. Benyus in her book, *BioMimicry: Innovation Inspired by Nature* describes the critical role of diversity in nature, providing us with a sustainable corporate model as well.

Of selecting seeds she says, "You are not only selecting for high yields, large seed size, uniform maturation time, easily threshed seeds, low shattering, winter hardiness, disease and pest resistance, and climate tolerance, but also for compatibility — a plant's ability to perform well or even exceed performance when grown next to other plants." The wonder, surprise, and payoff is that, "as nature has shown us, only polycultures are able to pay their own bills."[8]

Isn't that astounding? "…only polycultures are able to pay their own bills."

Collaboration thrives in a polyculture. Diversity allows for each encounter to be a little different from another. Once it's expected, it's less threatening. In fact, we start to welcome it.

Strong leaders know that innovation depends on diversity. To get lots of ideas, we need lots of perspectives. True things may get a bit messy. Maybe even uncomfortable. We may need to learn how to listen, set some ground rules, build up some tolerance. We'll need to listen rather than wait our turn. We'll know we've succeeded when saris and starched shirts not only eat at the same table but laugh together as well.

At *The Second City*, cast members are hired for talent but also for having a unique perspective. This can make writing and "living" together difficult at times.

---

[8]   Benyus, Janine M. *Biomimicry: Innovation Inspired By Nature*. 1997, reissued 2002. New York. Harper Perennial.

The players are passionate about different things. They don't even necessarily laugh at the same things. The one thing that brings them together is the search to "find the funny" in the truth.

Togetherness requires tolerance. At *The Second City*, we had no choice. We ate meals together and pranced in parades together. Because of the odd hours, we lost touch with family and friends. We became family and were together whether we liked it or not.

Just like family, we learned to accept the idiosyncrasies. These became notable especially moments before a show. Eric, the fast-talking, Guinness-drinking Brit, played with props. He would tape a doll's arm to his jacket and come in squealing that, "a light saber just shrunk my arm!" Margaret rested against the wall, reading and smoking a cigarette. Catherine primped. Larry tried to shock the women, and often did. Keegan made up words. Jacks wrote in his journal. I looked for food. Occasionally, we resorted to a game that involved kicking each other in the shins.

> **"When an improviser lets go** and trusts his fellow performers, it's a wonderful, liberating experience that stems from group support. A truly funny scene is not the result of someone trying to steal laughs at the expense of his partner, but of generosity — trying to make the other person (and his ideas) look as good as possible..."
> *Truth in Comedy*

When the stage manager yelled "Places!" we flew to our spots backstage, ready to perform our separate functions as one team.

If diversity invites innovation, we also know it invites resilience. Resilient companies thrive in the unpredictable economic landscape we find ourselves in today. In *The Beak of the Finch:* Weiner actually identifies the level of diversity required to thrive. "Take two species that come together. Say they differ by 10 percent. They would need to be about 15 percent different to coexist without serious competition. There are two possible outcomes. One of the two may go extinct, or the two species may diverge until they are 15 percent different. That shift is not very great: only another 5 percent."[9]

Ask yourself:
What would it take our company to be 15 percent different from our competitors?

A 15 percent difference within our team and from our competitor is a good indication of survival. It's certainly not a guarantee, but we can infer that a 10 percent difference, if we are to believe science, is a wide-open path to extinction.

It makes sense that branding experts, MBA programs, and business marketers stress the importance of finding a niche.

WHERE There's a whole science as to how environment affects collaboration so I'll just cite a few examples. Lew Epstein from Steelcase puts it this way. "For true collaboration, groups need spaces that nurture the process of collaboration. Work is not defined by what you do at a desk and organizations are no longer confined within office towers. Collaborative teams need comfortable, versatile collaborative spaces to work in."[10]

Similarly, *Making Room for Collaboration*,[11] a white paper published by Herman Miller, stresses four spacial features paramount to enhancing collaboration. These features include location, visual display, layouts, and traffic patterns along with balancing solitude and interaction.

The space used by the dschool at Stanford can adapt to the creative process as quickly as the ideas themselves. The flexible environment invites people to connect and play. The space becomes a partner to the innovators rather than one more obstacle to learning. The open environment is a radical as the collaboration itself.

---

9   Weiner, Jonathan. 2005. *The Beak of the Finch: A Story of Evolution in Our Time*. Vintage. First Vintage Books edition.

10   Epstein, Lew. *360 Research, Distributed Collaboration: Work's Future in View*. Issue 61. Steelcase, Inc.

11   *Making Room for Collaboration*. 2008. Herman Miller, Inc.

Contrast that to cubicles, one of the many office environments currently in use, which reinforce monoculture instead of the polyculture needed for collaboration.

How we got here is a testimonial to the 1950s suburban development. By catering to our comfort level, our yearning for sameness, we built entire cities with this model. We justified the movement by arguing for efficiency.

Farming used the same playbook. In Iowa, this looks like corn. Rows of corn. Miles of cornfields soaking up the sun. Stalks sway obediently, all reacting as one to the wind whipping through the plain. Beautiful. Orderly. And boring. From the interstate, by the time you enter Nebraska, you're wearing the sort of glazed look you develop in line at the Department of Motor Vehicles. The monotony is excruciating. Even a large anthill would be a nice reprieve.

We do the same at work. We put all the engineers in a nice quiet spot, we find a groovy setting for the designers, and we make sure all the executives can look out a window. The facilities crew is happy. It's efficient. Yet, the grouping eliminates the crosspollination needed for innovation.

To get the diversity that helps us adapt and thrive, we need to make boundaries more porous — boundaries between groups, projects, disciplines, and departments. We need to nourish a more organic approach to teamwork. We can then begin to experience a sustainable means of empowering teams to form and dissolve as needed.

It won't just be the food at the potluck that's different. It will be the people, the location, the food types, the utensils, and even the seating options. The result: a product or service providing your company with a unique position in the marketplace.

Observing who/what/where makes for better management, better teamwork, and better product development. The awareness invites proactive problem-solving. This really is the basis for human centered design. When you're cognizant of the needs of those around you, when you invite and respect diversity, the range of insights grows exponentially. So do the solutions. You have more information at your disposal so you make better decisions.

The improvisational tool of who/what/where helps you prepare for a presentation, calm a customer, improve processes, and ultimately, stay competitive.

Recently a research and development group asked for help generating greater empathy for customers. The developers resisted that emphasis on the customer, believing it would take too much time. They were concerned it would derail the project and run contrary to expertise. Surprisingly, the problem was just that. They were experts. Bright, well-trained and educated. They knew too much. The challenge was to move them away from their assumptions and purely logical approach.

Betty Edwards, in her book, *Drawing on the Right Side of the Brain*, reminds us that symbols get in the way of seeing.[12] We know what a chair looks like. We see them every day. In fact, we see them so often, we no longer see them at all. The brain substitutes a symbol as shorthand. The symbol improves efficiency. If we truly saw everything in front of us every day, we would shut down from overstimulation. We need the symbols most of the time.

When the marketplace calls for improved functionality, however, we need designers to see the chair. We need them to move past the symbol. To create a better potato peeler, product developers need to forget everything they know about potatoes. This is especially hard to do if you like, say, French fries. It's the only way though if they want to "fix" the potato peeler.

---

12   Edwards, Betty. *Drawing on the Right Side of the Brain*. 1979. Harper Collins Publishers.

The "who" is no longer a generic term, the who is the individual right in front of you. In the case of the potato peeler, you see the user's hands, arthritic, struggling to grasp the tiny handle.

The "what" means slowing down to observe behavior, listening to personal stories, and empathizing with frustrations. Taking time to Yes, And! what is, rather than what you believe should be.

> **"I've learned that I still have a lot to learn**...I've learned that people will forget what you said, people will forget what you did, but people will never forget how you made them feel."
> *Maya Angelou*

The "where" provides the context. You no longer assume people only use a potato peeler at a kitchen sink, all the while picturing your own kitchen and your own sink. You now see how and where this person actually uses your product. It may even be at their kitchen sink, but chances are, especially in different cultures, the shape and placement of that sink is quite different from your own.

PLAY LIST
- Who
  - Step inside some other shoes
  - When people show you who they are, believe them
  - Share the blame and the glory
- What
  - Make peace with the elephants
  - Play in polycultures
  - When you're hungry, change your beak
- Where
  - Make space for play
  - Slow down and see

7

Yes, And! Give and Take

The trouble with her is that she lacks the power of conversation but not the power of speech.
George Bernard Shaw

Ever get caught at lunch next to someone who just won't stop talking? What about the neighbor who asks to borrow your mower, your weed whacker, your car? They talk. You listen. They talk. You daydream. They continue to talk and you — retreat, explode, lie, or worse.

It's similar to being in a relationship with someone who gives gifts but is no good at receiving them. At first, it's wonderful. They remember your birthday, your anniversary, the day you stopped smoking. After awhile however you start to feel pressured. You like them. You like getting gifts. You just can't keep up. It starts to feel competitive. You can't afford the money or the time. It's not that you don't like them. It's just that the giving is disproportionate. The relationship is out of balance. Eventually, the imbalance damages the relationship. This happens on stage, at home, and at work.

A comfortable level of give and take creates an ensemble, a team. Members feel equal. Each individual finds a way to contribute and is open to the contribution of others. The balance creates a comfort level that allows for collaboration.

You're Not Alone

You've seen improvisers on stage and on TV. Maybe you have taken an improv class or workshop. What they have in common is that there is more than one person participating. This doesn't mean that you can't use the tools on your own. It just means that for greatest effectiveness and to enhance solutions, your ability to cooperate and collaborate with others is paramount.

Here's what's great about all of this. If you take an intentional approach to improvisation, you will not work alone. The skill requires people to put aside their own interests and needs and wants in favor of the group. It requires a setting aside of

> **"Play, as free improvisation,** sharpens our capacity to deal with a changing world."
> *Stephen Nachmanovitch*

self to know the whole. Improvisation creates a true team only if each member thinks first and predominantly of the other person. It causes you to ask: What gifts can I give the others? How can I make them look good? What is the best choice for everyone and not just for me?

Improvisation is by nature collaborative. So is business.

Big Feet, Big Lessons

The right amount of giving and taking on stage makes for great entertainment. The performance seems effortless and the interplay magical. The magic begins off stage; giving ideas that help build a character, offering suggestions to improve scenes, and sharing stories that matter. Players give encouragement, feedback, and, sometimes, half of a hamburger. The better players are at sharing...almost everything, the better the show.

Player's give and take props, costumes, information, and focus. They give tips on how to make scenes better. They show rookies how to read running orders and handle hecklers. Yet all players, at all levels, have to share. It can't be one sided. Too much giving or taking on the part of any one player throws off the balance. Even rookies have to find ways to contribute and let go.

Each player in an ensemble must be generous enough to give gifts. He or she also must be willing to give over to the other players. This may mean giving up control, an agenda for a scene, a beloved character that doesn't fit, or a funny line that gets a laugh but kills the scene.

Each must be also be courageous enough to take when necessary. This may mean speaking up or jumping in. It may mean entering a scene even if the director didn't cast them in the scene. If a player can save a scene from dying, her job is to jump on stage and make it work. She doesn't worry about how she looks or if it was in the job description. She doesn't worry about the consequences for a promotion or demotion. She takes the risk because she sees a need and knows she must meet the need, now. It can be terrifying. Worse though, would be waiting in the wings watching others suffer. That isn't fair to them or the audience. The great improviser is as generous at giving as they are at taking.

Of course, people are human and sometimes give too much or take too soon. It happens.

Most of us though when it comes to relationships think of taking negatively. We think of taking as selfish, needy, and small minded. We speak as if taking is the opposite of generosity. One person had something of value and another person took it. If done to the detriment of another performer, the scene, or even the audience, performers describe the behavior as stealing. The act may get a laugh but it does so at the expense of something or someone else. Rather than raising everyone's profile, the action raises one person's profile and lowers everybody else's.

Unfortunately, this language, this perception, causes people to have a narrow view of taking. It doesn't work on stage or in the office. It implies that dependence is bad and asking for help is weak. The false "high-mindedness" destroys effective teamwork.

As you know, sometimes the best lessons come from when things don't work. One former fellow cast member taught me a lot what not to do on stage, especially when it came to giving and taking.

Trevor was great at taking. Not so great at giving. He knew how to get a laugh, raise his profile, and steal the scene. Trevor had thick wrists, thick ankles, and enormous feet...or at least enormous shoes. He was the first person I met on my first day of performing with a new troupe. On a break, he offered me to lunch. Nice. Then I realized he wanted control. He wanted to be the first to tell me how things really worked. He said he was going to "show me the ropes."

His efforts seemed intended to intimidate me and they worked. The restaurant was dark and fancy. He smoked and talked and looked like he'd skipped bowling league to meet with me and I'd better appreciate the sacrifice. When he finally stopped talking, I realized he also expected me to pay for the meal. I did.

Later that evening, after the show, he reviewed his performance. Apparently, it was masterful. I have to admit he was talented. In fact, he was definitely one of the better players - quick, high-energy, and smart.

He could also be difficult. In one of my first shows, one particular scene required me to run across the stage, encounter scary figures on the way, and have conversations with them. I ran past one ghost after another until I reached Trevor, the last person in the way of this character's arrival to safety out of scary-land. He played a street person asleep near a dumpster. When I ran toward him, the scene called for him to jump in front of me, scare me, and say something profound. Each time we practiced the scene, however, he didn't like where I ran. He said I was ruining his object work. He pointed out an imaginary telephone pole and dumpster. I tried running in different directions to different places. It seemed that the alley kept changing size and the objects grew larger each time we practiced.

I was new and nervous. I focused on my performance. I clearly didn't understand the value and importance of object work. I didn't take the time to see the scene as Trevor did. Although it wasn't intentional on my part, looking back, my guess is that he may have interpreted this as a sign of disrespect. In the green room, just minutes before the show, he quietly told me that if I ran in the wrong spot he would jump out and land on both of my feet. I coughed up a fake laugh. He didn't crack a smile.

The scene got off to a great start. I started to relax. We were having fun and the audience was right with us. Then came the part I'd been dreading. I ran across the stage, and though I looked hard to see exactly what Trevor was seeing, I must not have. He jumped out and, true to his word, landed those big, black hard-soled shoes squarely on both my feet. He did so looking straight at me. I gasped. I couldn't breathe. My eyes filled from the pain. I squeaked out my line and hobbled off stage.

After the show he came over to me and said, "I told you that if you ran in the wrong spot, I would have to jump on you. Don't make me do it again."

What surprised me most was that the stage we were playing on was huge. That alley could have been any shape and size we wanted. We both had the freedom to create the environment and the objects. The objective was to play an entertaining scene for the audience - one that would make them laugh and think. Our goal was not to create a specific setting. The setting was to support the scene, not be the scene. Trevor and I were limited only by our choices of what to see and play. We were also limited by our ability to work together, to give and take generously.

We had choices. We also had an obligation to share the vision and make the scene work. We both failed.

> **"The only road** to strength is vulnerability."
> Stephen Nachmanovitch

I've been on stage with both types of people, those who give gifts and make you look great, and those who steal focus and destroy the scene. I've performed with players who leave you energized and those who make you panic. I've watched players refuse to engage because of fear, lack of focus, or laziness. I've also witnessed generosity that rivals Mother Teresa.

The kind of taking I'm talking about requires self-confidence and attentiveness. It requires the player to listen and be sensitive to the needs of others in the moment. The kind of taking I'm talking about is sacrificial. It requires taking a risk, letting go, and trusting the other players. This kind of taking results in a culture that, no matter what happens to you, no matter what choices you make, no matter how bad your breath, people still want you around.

Positive give and take requires a balance that results in a free exchange of ideas and solutions. Everyone is involved in voicing ideas. The discoveries are communal. The solutions belong to the group.

Sharing the burden, making others look good, and giving gifts are all part of the natural interchange of a strong working team.

Make Assumptions

Giving gifts requires making assumptions. That seems odd doesn't it? It seems most times we discourage making assumptions. We're taught that it's more polite to ask questions rather than assume.

Here's the problem with questions. When you ask someone a question, you may believe you are showing interest. Actually, you are asking the other person to do the work. They answer the question, and then, typically, you ask a follow-up. This allows you to steer the conversation in a direction most comfortable for you. It allows you to remain passive in a sense and it requires no transparency on your part. It also forces them to talk about what interests you.

By contrast, an assumption makes a statement. The other person can enter the conversation using that statement at any juncture. The statement requires you to provide some transparency, thus making the other person more comfortable. You've given a little, which means you've given them permission to give a little back. An assumption requires you to be a keen observer of nonverbal behavior, the environment, and the relationships in the room. Assumptions do require more work on your part but often lead to more comfortable and more revealing conversations more quickly.

In my coaching, since new leaders typically start attending more events, they ask for tips on "small talk." Their boss expects they know how to handle these situations. They know it's important. Ability to handle these informal events increases visibility, credibility, and leverage.

The unexpected is often seen, at best, as an unwelcome distraction, or at worst, a major derailing factor, resulting in panic and poor decision-making.

We hope people leave the event talking of our storytelling ability, or our amazing adventures, or our insight. Unfortunately, our discomfort makes us forgettable. We end up playing it safe. We focus on ourselves and not on others.

The easiest way to create a good impression and to make you more comfortable is to take initiative, make the assumption, and create a more comfortable atmosphere for the other person. Once you make the observation or assumption, you get to listen. This may actually be the hard part. You must remain quiet long enough to provide them with a choice as to how and when to enter the conversation.

By doing so, you allow them to share information at a level of depth, intimacy, and detail of their own choosing. You get to build on these assumptions as well. You get to discover connections and Yes, And! them.

A perfect place to practice this is in the elevator. Instead of looking down and waiting for the door to open, observe the other person(s.) Little observations open doors.

Consider the difference:

Questions	Assumptions
How are you?	Downtown seems busier today than usual.
What do you do for _____ company?	You seem to know this place quite well. I'm assuming this isn't your first time here.
Have you been in town long?	This is my first time in [city]. I'm impressed by [art, architecture, night life, quiet...].
How long have your worked for _____ company?	This [room, painting, meal] reminds me of [vacation, family, work situation] because...
Are you married? Children?	My [spouse, significant other] would be especially [surprised by, interested in] the...because...
Are you ready for your presentation in the morning?	The presentation earlier made me wonder about...

Assumptions are different from planned responses. A planned response doesn't allow you to react to what's actually being said. Instead, you're merely waiting your turn. You have an agenda. You have something to say and will say it regardless of what's happening now. You aren't listening. You're missing opportunities. You're cheating the other person and yourself. It may feel more comfortable to you at the time, but forcing an idea or comment into a conversation is at best awkward and at worst downright disrespectful.

Unfortunately, too many times we miss the opportunity because we are sticking so rigidly to our plan for the day, the month, the year. We have forms for conducting interactions, scripts for talking to each other, and a company manual entry for any given procedure. If it's not on our checklist, we don't do it. But that is all planning. The problem with it comes when the customer, in the moment, presents us with an opportunity we didn't expect. Now what? For many of us, we choose to resist that opportunity because we are uncertain, and stick to what we do know.

We may still make the sale, complete the phone call, or add a contact to our database, but we've squandered an opportunity for future interactions or more innovative solutions to customer needs. Who knows, we might even have lost an opportunity to create a product design way ahead of our competition. Ignoring these little moments, these not-so-insignificant daily events, can result in our loss of market share and our ability to lead with confidence.

> **Ask yourself:**
> How do I demonstrate my expertise to the customer?

Of course, you still plan and prepare for these moments ahead of time. The difference is that once you're prepared, you let go. You remain flexible. You're open-minded.

When you do engage, be sure you're allowing for interaction. On stage, we're careful not to give too much information at once. We pause so that the other players have a chance to build on what they've heard, or seen. The same is true in conversation. Pausing allows for a genuine give and take. The connections develop more quickly. The relationship deepens and, it's a lot more fun.

The Customer

We do this with customers. We're so anxious to tell them everything about our product that we don't hear their real need. Once we get rolling, we can't get ourselves to stop. We're so excited to use the words we've learned, our fancy terminology, that we lose them after the first few minutes. "We have a CRM that interfaces with a variety of platforms, one of which…"

The other extreme is to act as if "the customer is always right." The danger here is that we don't share our expertise. We gain consumer insights but we don't lead with solutions. They start wondering why they spent so much time showing you the plant, highlighting case studies, and explaining their processes.

Customers expect us to know something they don't. They assume you know more than they do and so, not only can you provide immediate solutions, you also can anticipate needs. You can initiate a strategic approach that will help them reach their goals. You can provide insights that, because they're so close to the situation, they can't see.

To implement true give and take, we Yes, And! consumer motives, moods, interests, pain, obstacles and anything else they bring our way. We take the time to know and understand the culture. Customers don't always know what they need or want, and they don't even always know why they need or want it. That's why getting in touch with their pain, understanding their need is so critical.

At the same time, you build trust. Now you can provide tailored recommendations that genuinely meet their needs.

It also can save you both a lot of time. Sometimes, after getting to know them better, you realize there's not a fit at all. You get to recommend another vendor who can meet their needs and preserve your brand at the same time.

Back Story

I learned about give and take during one of my first rehearsals after joining *The Second City*. These early rehearsals stretched me in ways I never expected. I learned about the tools of improvisation in short order.

We, the new cast, were all lying on our backs in the dark in the rehearsal room — a fancy name for a large, half-remodeled space used to store extra chairs and empty kegs. I'm pretty sure the floor had never been

> **"The key task for leaders** is to explore and innovate in chaotic conditions. Essentially, an organization must be flexible enough to adapt, creative enough to innovate, and responsive enough to learn."
> *Organizational Dynamics Magazine*

vacuumed. The director, Rico, instructed us to close our eyes. We obeyed. He then asked us to start telling a story and off we went. We took turns jumping in and taking the story in a different direction each time. I liked it a lot at first — the story was funny and interesting. Then, someone ended the story, or so I thought. Apparently, another cast member thought differently and started up again. This happened at least five times. Why wasn't Rico stopping this mess? Wasn't he listening? Surely, he must know the story ended. He had the authority to stop us. Why wasn't he using it?

I started to get agitated and bored. I wasn't the only one. I could hear the loud breathing. The sighing. The story became ridiculous, and he still didn't stop us. It went on forever. It ate up our entire rehearsal. I thought I'd never get off that floor. Finally, someone just blurted out, "The end." It was completely out of context. It wasn't a natural ending but we were so glad she ended it that we didn't care. Rico flipped on the lights and smiled his huge smile. I was not smiling.

I had a lot at stake. I didn't have time to lie around on my back and listen to a terrible story. In college, I majored in English. I taught English for many years. I knew what made a good story. I knew about exposition, inciting impulse, rising action, climax, and denouement. I could even diagram and label it on the board to teach others.

Maybe the issue was that Rico didn't know the components of a good story. Although, given his career accomplishments, this seemed unlikely. Perhaps he didn't prepare for rehearsal so he just let that go on and on so we wouldn't have to do anything else.

Then, with a wry smile and professorial tone, he asked, "How did that go?" People gave some answers about content and character. And then he asked, "Are you happy with the story?" I was exhausted. Since these first couple months were with the touring company, I was still teaching during the day. It wasn't until I moved to the main stage that I could quit my job and do this full time.

This meant I'd been up since 6:00 a.m., taught ninth-graders all day, graded papers in the back seat while Jacks, another touring company member, drove the car until we did a "drive by" for a fish filet. From that point on, we practiced scenes for the show until we arrived at the dark, cold theater.

Understandably, I wanted an answer to this story thing and to go home. I waited for what I thought was an appropriate amount of time and then asked, "Rico, why didn't you end the story?" He smiled.

"Why would I end it?

"Because you're the director and I'm sure you could tell the story was over."

"Could you tell the story was over?" he asked.

"Of course."

"How did you know?"

"Because it stopped making any sense. It got boring," I said ever so articulately.

"Do the rest of you agree?"

They nodded. He asked the group, "So why didn't any of you end the story?"

Others chimed in. "Because it seemed like each time we were getting to the end, someone would start it up again. Take it in a new direction."

"Uh huh."

"So, we were figuring you would stop us when we got to the end like that."

"Why would I stop you?"

"Because you're the director."

"And?"

"So, it's your job to stop us. Plus, the story got dumb and we were just wasting time. Don't we have a lot to rehearse for Friday's show?"

"Uh huh."

This was starting to drive me crazy. Now we had to guess why we were wasting time. Unbelievable.

He paused. Finally, he said, "If I stopped you, how would you know when you came to the end?" He paused again. "I can't be up there on stage with you. You have to be able to end the scene yourselves. If you sensed the story was over, why didn't you end it?"

I chimed in, "Because I didn't know we were supposed to. I thought you were going to do it."

"You needed permission? Why was that?"

"I wanted to make sure I was doing it right. You didn't tell us we could end it." I realized the conversation was starting to go in circles.

Again Rico, "You were trying to please me. Improvisation is about finding the answers together. You shouldn't need someone from the outside telling you what to do. You need to listen to yourself and your team member. Strive to discover what the story needs, the character needs, or your fellow team member needs. If I, or anyone else, tell you how, you will never have the confidence to find it yourself. Plus, it would be pretty strange if I jumped into the show to tell you to enter a scene, exit a scene or yell, 'Hey, scene's over. The end.'"

"Okay. I understand. Now, about Friday night's show, when are we going to rehearse since we're out of time tonight?

"We just did." Rico continued, "Knowing how to work as an ensemble, how to listen for the story and the focus of the story, and knowing when and how to edit are all skills you need to do this work. We are rehearsing. As a team, we'll get better at this."

I still had a little fight in me. "Okay, but still, you have to admit it would be more efficient if you just told us this is what we were supposed to learn."

"If I told you what to learn, the learning wouldn't stick with you. You won't forget this. Am I right?"

Yes. He was right.

He cleverly employed what we call discovery learning. If you discover the lesson yourself, you are more likely to internalize the learning. For lasting behavioral and culture change, this works. It feels cumbersome and time-consuming. In the long run, however, if the learning sticks, ultimately you've saved yourself a lot of time. Invest early for the greatest return.

> **"What's particularly appealing** about improvisation is its basic tenet: nothing gets rejected... The lesson is: Don't be afraid to go out and risk it. The tragedy is to play it safe."
> *The Wall Street Journal*

Elmer's Glue

Remember second grade? I do. It was a tough year. I wasn't as cute as I was in kindergarten when I could readily claim any adult lap as my own. I also wasn't tall enough to ride the rollercoaster. On top of this, my second grade teacher, Mrs. Lutz, singled me out to teach the class a lesson.

One day, when I was deeply invested in some primary research, she barked, "Mary Jane, what is that on your hand?"

Focused on my work, I heard nothing.

She said it again. This time sounds got through but no meaning. "Mary Jane, fiehaoo doowyast ghhastt eieilleri hand?"

Then, once more, loud enough for the entire subdivision to hear. I looked up. There she was, in the room with me, right next to my desk in fact.

"I will say this one more time. Mary Jane, what is on your hand?"

"Elmer's glue."

"I see that."

Oh brother. Then why was she bothering me?

"Mary Jane, no one is to be using glue now. We are reading a story."

I look up at her blankly. That's fine I thought. You guys can read a story. I don't mind.

She continued. "You will not waste school resources by pouring them on your hand."

Oh. Now it makes sense. She doesn't understand. I should explain. "I'm not wasting it. I'm eating it." Perfect, I think. Now that my intentions are clear we can all get back to what we're doing.

It was, however, in that moment, our worlds collided. This would be the first of many meaningful interchanges with Mrs. Lutz. Unfortunately, it took most of the year to try to sort out our differences. We didn't have the luxury of ignoring each other. We were stuck together that year — like glue. It felt like a long year.

That's when I realized, ignoring just doesn't work. It takes a lot of energy. It certainly is more tiring than taking action. With Mrs. Lutz, my denial did not make anything go away. In fact, it made things worse. The pinnacle was the day I peed in my chair. Yes. It was intentional. Rather than try to explain to Mrs. Lutz that my bladder couldn't wait until recess, I peed in my seat. I thought my tartan skirt would absorb the liquid more efficiently. Essentially I learned two lessons that day. One about relationships. The other about textiles.

Ownership

A final story on give and take brings up the complexity of ownership. *The Second City* takes a radical approach. No surprise. Here's how I learned the lesson. Although I'd been improvising for several years before I joined the cast of *The Second City*, I didn't realize the full significance give and take would have on my contributions to the team.

After a particularly energizing rehearsal, the cast left, charged to put some of the amazing scene ideas we discovered to paper. I was excited and wrote for a couple hours. I carried copies of my scene into rehearsal my name proudly appearing just under the title of the scene. After all, from kindergarten on up, each teacher required it.

The director surprised me when he said, "Mary Jane, we do not put our names on the scenes we write."

Surprised, I responded, "What? How will you know then who wrote the scene?"

"Who wrote the scene is not important." Incredulous, I just stared at him. He continued, "Once you bring a scene to the rest of the cast, you are no longer the 'owner' of that scene. The scene now belongs to all of us."

I'd studied Communism, and even lived communally. This sounded very similar but it sure didn't sound like good business. Wouldn't we want to know who owned the piece? How would we know who to praise or promote if the scene went well? Who would we blame if the scene went poorly?

Obviously, I missed his point. With improvisation, true ownership means we win and lose together. We all take responsibility for each decision, idea, and performance. This truly was revolutionary to me. It can be revolutionary to your business as well. As Charna Halpern says, "You bring a brick, and I bring a brick. Then together, we build a house."

It is complicated though when it comes to business. Most companies conduct yearly performance reviews based on individual productivity.. Yes they tell you to work as a team. Yes, they are enamored with the word "collaboration." Ultimately though, you rise or fall once a year on your own merit.

Of course individuals do make a difference. In fact, so much so, that some companies carry the names of their founders. Consider Henry Ford, Harley-Davidson, and Christian Dior. Of course, this is not always the case. Bill Gates is pivotal to the company yet we refer to it as Microsoft.

As in most things, how to balance individual contribution with team effort is not clean or easy. The solution is complex. It's probably somewhere in between. If we are willing to investigate the nuance, avoid a one-size-fits-all solution, and talk openly about it with our teams however, the tension can actually be energizing, even motivating.

The bigger question really is how do you nurture a culture that invites pride of ownership from every contributor? Rewarding the few certainly won't work. Taking away individual responsibility won't work either.

When teams collaborate effectively, they find things in common. Individuals want to be part of the outcome. They want to be involved in the process early. They say Yes, And! to each other and welcome a diversity of opinion. The give and take encourages the dynamic culture required for innovation. Specific, Measurable, Attainable, Realistic, and Time-Sensitive (S.M.A.R.T.)[13] goals help them achieve positive outcomes.

Rewarding individual contributors doesn't go away, but too much of it robs your company from the breadth and depth of your employees' creativity. We still celebrate contributions, reward hard work, and ensure accountability. We're careful to balance individual success with that of the group. It's a fine line. One you'll have to monitor and adjust often.

Improvisation is a great leveler. It's not the titles that count, it's the contribution.

PLAY LIST
→ Share the entire stage
→ Be generous
→ Make assumptions
→ Stop when the story's over
→ Share the scene

13   Doran, G.T. (1981). "There's a S.M.A.R.T. way to write management's goals and objectives." *Management Review*, Volume 70, Issue 11 (AMA FORUM), pp. 35-36.

8

Yes, And! Commit

Take time to deliberate but when the time for action arrives,
stop thinking and go in.
Andrew Jackson

In improvisation, there are no right or wrong answers. To some that's liberating. To others it's unnerving. DeWitt Jones in his glorious film, "Creativity," reminds us that there is always more than one right answer. Maybe you prefer to think of it that way. Still, at some point we have to choose an answer. We'll never have enough time to do all the research we'd like. We'll never have enough money or time for the perfect solution. We must make a choice, go forward, and take action. Doing so is liberating. Taking action erases the apathy that saps our energy. Is there the potential for failure? Yes. We know, however, "If you do nothing, you'll be nothing."

Failure

To be fair, it's important to remind you that failure is a big part of this analogy. Improvisation not only encourages risk-taking that may lead to failure, it requires it.

Applied improvisation requires the same kind of intelligent discipline you would require of any other methodology. I am not suggesting you move into the future with a cavalier approach to failure. We all know that no matter how diligent we are with our decisions, any movement or adaptation carries with it a level of uncertainty. Any step toward growth carries with it a certain level of pain.

Any level of failure, at its very least, will be uncomfortable. And with good reason. Failure makes us look bad. When we look bad, others look better. When we look bad, we have to admit we have faults or cover up the truth. We also have to admit we don't have all the answers.

Improvisation requires a willingness to look foolish. If people allow themselves to look foolish, they can ultimately be more successful in the long run. You've heard the phrase, "Fail early and often." Discover the options and you'll find more than one right answer.

Failure also requires the kind of trust built on honesty. The team must recognize they can't do it alone. They must give themselves over, immerse themselves in the process. They must ask for help. They must be vulnerable in the moment. They must be willing to explore and learn.

What does this look like in a volatile economic environment? It means sticking to your mission while exploring options to your business plan. It means entertaining the wild ideas from the guy with the funny glasses. It means listening to a customer who has a story to tell. It means improvising to manage change successfully with confidence, humor, and flexibility.

Heart and Soul

Rico, our producer at *The Second City*, said, "I've got your soul in this drawer." He opened the drawer on his right. I peered in. There it was. A 3x5 card scrawled with the words, "Your soul" stared back at me. I was in his office to renew my contract. We did this every four months. He would call us in, one at a time, toy with us, flash a smile, and then we'd sign.

I looked at him. I had no idea what I was supposed to say. I thought he might be trying to be funny, except he never did that. He never tried to be funny. Rico, a true improviser at heart, told the truth.

What freaked me out was that after eight months of working full-time at *The Second City*, Rico was offering me another contract to do another show. My job, as before, would be to write the next show and perform it seven times a week. It also included performing the five improv sets a week. Along with that, I taught at the training center. On Mondays, our theater's "dark" day, I would perform corporate shows. In my spare time, I marched in parades, shot short films, and taped a TV series.

> **"Until one is committed**, there is hesitancy, the chance to draw back, always ineffectiveness... Whatever you can do or dream you can, begin it. Boldness has genius, power and magic in it. Begin it now." *Goethe*

I was thrilled he was offering me the job again, but this was a strange twist. He had a knack for keeping people off balance. The walls of his office were purple and he had the program covers of all the shows he had been in framed and hanging on the wall. He asked me again if I wanted to sign the contract and reminded me with the 3x5 card that he had my soul in his drawer. I got it. The job was more than the words on that contract. The job was even more than performing all those shows. The job required that to perform those shows, I had to put my "soul" into every scene I wrote. The audience needed to see my "soul" on stage in every character I played. I had to place my "soul" into the arms of the ensemble.

This job required me to tell the truth, to speak up for what I believed, and somehow to "find the funny" so others would listen.

Stop Trying So Hard

Allow yourself some room to be wrong. The harder you try, the more anxious you will be. The harder you try, the more you will find that you are imitating others or trying to fit into a norm. That's like trying to be how tall you are.

Remember, you are original because there is no one else exactly like you. Embrace the snowflake phenomenon. It's true with humans too and even more interesting.

Start spending time with yourself. Relax. Allow yourself those crazy thoughts you have and set out on a journey. Explore them. Live with them. Just like the elephants, take them out to dinner.

Surround yourself with people who like you for who you are and not your position, your money, or your influence. Surround yourself with people who let you be exactly who you are.

Remember when you ran outside, grabbed a stick, and became sheriff of the town? Or when you put tights under your puffy pajamas, picked up your tin foil wand, and turned a frog into a prince? You didn't wait for someone to tell you your wand wouldn't work. You just waved it. You had confidence because you believed you could. It was that simple and, in many ways, it still is.

Executive Presence

Committing to the moment and acting on the decision can also teach us a lot about executive presence. It's not that executives don't ever get nervous, or that they always know just how to act, or that the audience is in the dark. That's some of it but, there's a lot more. It's that belief that this moment is real and that the only option is to throw yourself completely into it. Doubt isn't on the invitation list to this party. Again, it's like when you were young. You just did it and it was 100 percent real to you — and to the kids you were playing with. This kind of play seems to be a lost art. Unfortunately, we experience thousands more losses because of it. But it's not too late to get it back. The only requirement is that you resume that belief, that passion again, 100 percent. We will never believe you

> **"The basic difference** between an ordinary man and a warrior is that a warrior takes everything as a challenge while an ordinary man takes everything either as a blessing or a curse."
> *Carlos Castanada*

unless you believe it yourself. And if you don't, if you're not passionate about what you're doing, you'll lose focus and you'll lose us.

You gain executive presence through the tools of improvisation, giving you the confidence and joy that makes other people want to sit near you, listen to you, and buy you lunch. The first step is to believe you have it. That's right. Just believe and act on that belief.

Perhaps you can even think about what you wear as the props and costumes for the "show." It's not about creating a facade. It's about bringing out what's already inside and doing so with confidence and, maybe even, flair. You certainly can find your own style but, just as a good speaker knows her audience, you need to dress in a way that inspires confidence in you and your product.

Your job is the same. Your job is to make yourself, your team and your customer feel completely at home the minute you meet. When you show up to meet your customer, make their place of work your own. Begin by demonstrating that you know enough about them to talk intelligently and that you have a comfort level with them and their business. If you are uncomfortable, they will be too. The more quickly you can break the ice and share a laugh, the better. Executive presence has everything to do with being comfortable in your own skin.

Your ability to increase the comfort level between yourself and others is critical to developing strong relationships. Out of these strong relationships develops the trust that is so important in every business interaction. Take time to learn about others and display the sensitivity that others require. Good manners go far beyond just being nice. Good manners can take you to new levels in your relationships with others.

Is that an example of executive presence? I think so. Beyond all the suggestions about clothes, posture, and eye contact, the undeniable passion in what you are doing, the willingness to look foolish, the readiness to take a risk at the right time allow you to command the room in a positive way. Remember, 80 percent of communication is nonverbal. How you act and behave is far more important than what you say. Think content vs. delivery.

Beyond the Passion

Passion encourages commitment. When we're passionate, it shows. Our voice changes, our body tenses, we move more, our face is flushed. Body language tells people how you feel without uttering one word. On stage, performers who float upstage away from the audience and avoid eye contact appear under confident and low-status. Slumped shoulders, nondescript hand motions, and weak vocals communicate the same thing. Sometimes, during a performance, if there's too much of this on stage, stronger actors might just produce an "improvised" gun and put the weak player out of his misery. Very Darwinian. When one person is uncomfortable, we are distracted and uncomfortable. We know the audience is, too. As humans, we typically act quickly to avoid that which makes us uncomfortable.

To avoid being killed off in a scene, or at a sales call, you need to exude a strong sense of presence. You need to demonstrate that nothing is accidental. Everything is intentional. Be ready for anything. Show confidence. Make eye contact. Shake hands. By the way, don't show off by crushing bones, just shake the hand. Walk tall and start the conversation whenever you can. Observe the room — make it yours.

Meet Less, Do More

Stop commenting and start acting. Another way to say this is stop meeting and start doing. Meetings are the biggest timewasters we have, yet they are as deceptive as a siren song. We look busy and important but, most of the time, nothing of real value is happening other than we're allowed to procrastinate a bit longer. One client tracked the amount of time she spent in meetings in one month. She was shocked when she found it was 67 hours! Unfortunately, her schedule was not atypical.

Don't meet if you need an update, a review, or a report. This can happen easily in an e-mail or on intranet. Most of our meeting time falls into this category so we can quickly claim back many productive hours.

Do meet when you need to make a decision, when you need to build a relationship, when you need to brainstorm. One way to know whether to meet is if you can enter with a clear agenda that requires interaction and exit with a plan of action. (Even improvisers have a running order for the show.)

Don't underestimate how helpful this can be as you seek to connect with people at all levels in your company. One of the most obvious places we connect, or don't connect, is in meetings.

> **If people leave the meeting** committed to a next step toward a goal, the meeting is valuable.

Unfortunately, at times we get caught in aimless, unproductive meetings. This often happens when the attendees are unclear about the purpose or their roles. That, or they're not empowered to act. When this happens, we end up with a bunch of people who are too terrified to do anything.

See if you recognize these behaviors:

- The invitation goes out to everyone and anyone. This way everyone is "involved" and no one takes responsibility.
- Attendees ask who, how, and why questions but recoil from action.
- Attendees are passive. They either don't engage or allow one person to do all the talking.
- They guard their ideas.
- Their nonverbal behavior indicates a lack of engagement and energy.

The problem is that everyone acts like they're coming to class and someone else is the teacher. They look around directionless. Breathe a sigh of relief when they see the coffee and muffins. "Oh look, two liters of pop, too." This is really the reason people come to meetings. The food. It's fun to pick out ice cubes with tongs, pour a little Coke in the cup, and watch it fizz. Finally, a few moments in your day when you are not in charge. You relax into a black leather make-you-feel important chair and start scanning the room. You know some of these people, at least enough to nod at them and go back to your muffin.

You're just settling in for a good daydream when someone calls your name and asks you to report on some aspect of the project you've never heard of. You thought you heard words like "ancillary" and "specs," then you hear the word "priority." You're screwed. You look down at your black valise. It's leather, has your business card, and a pad of paper. (It's the same kind of thing you carried around in seventh grade except then it was a blue spiral notebook adorned with maniacal doodles.) If you carried it into class each day, you at least appeared prepared.

Since you're not sure what the question was, or even if it was a question, you respond with, "Yes, exactly. I'm concerned as well." Nice. Now the two of you are comrades. You've assured him he's not in it alone. "The stats are not quite ready yet. I've been up to my eyeballs in work, but I'm sure we can get you a report later today." All good. You've been on it. You've just been held up by someone else's inefficiency but you demonstrate compassion. Excellent. Plus you promise to get on it this afternoon, which is fine because we all know the meeting won't produce any results so you might even be ahead of the game. Once more for good measure. "My apologies. But to get you the most accurate numbers, I really need until later today." Phew. The heat is off, at least for awhile. The focus shifts across the table to Brian, who is new and sweating. Too bad for him.

The other option is not to meet at all. With this option, you can stay in your office until you need a haircut. The problem with that is that no one knows you're working. Even worse, they might give the credit to someone else. In light of this, showing up at the meeting is a better option. Maybe you should just have a snack and get back to work, like you did in kindergarten. In kindergarten, we got a lot done and still had a yummy snack. After that, it was out to the slide and then time to throw rocks at stuff.

Ask yourself:
How much time can be saved if we planned our meetings more carefully? If we used a meeting checklist?

Cynical perhaps, but I've been watching this weird meeting dance for a long time. We have a strange relationship with meetings. People complain about them a lot, but we just seem to add more, and they're longer than ever. Employees are scared to death and figure having meetings is a way to protect their jobs. And yet, many of those who sat in these boardrooms at the beautifully shaped wood tables no longer work in the company. The table is still there, but they're not.

Decide and Do

Commit to your choices completely and do so with integrity. When you waver, we wonder.

This doesn't mean you can't be flexible, but it does mean that at some point, you stop talking and take action.

Fear of failure keeps us from realizing our dreams, from telling the truth, from living in the moment. Unfortunately, it is through failure that we discover the right solutions, learn the truths about ourselves, and learn to move in a more satisfying direction.

Don't get me wrong. I hate to fail. Hate it. I want top scores on my evaluations, just like you. I want standing ovations every time I talk. I want people to wait in line to tell me how I've changed their lives. I want people laughing so hard at my shows that they can't breathe.

We all want that, and sometimes, if we're fortunate, it happens. Most of the time though the reaction is more muted. People clap appreciatively, thank me for my presentation, even refer me to others. All good.

Sometimes though, at the end of the event, people just leave. I don't get "all 5s" on an evaluation. My calls aren't returned. It stings.

I make mistakes. I misjudge a venue. I try out a new opener. I share my excitement for an idea that gets ignored. I spend thousands of dollars on a strategic plan only to realize it's the wrong direction.

I understand. Failing sucks. It's tempting to curl up, quiet down, and stay safe. But I can't imagine eating Cream of Wheat® every day. It's nourishing but boring. I don't want to miss out on the Bang Bang Shrimp.

Too much waiting and fretting means we miss out. We'll bitterly watch another person seize the moment, the position, the project.

Improvisation is about doing — now. We can pretend we're the fastest, smartest, and cleverest but until we try, we will never know.

PLAY LIST
→ Find lots of right answers
→ Free up failure
→ Take your soul to work
→ Stand tall and wave your wand
→ Start now

PART THREE: ACT

ACT at the highest level —
have courage—start now

9

Yes, Let's Get Started

Always leave enough time in your life to do something that makes you happy, satisfied, even joyous. That has more of an effect on economic well-being than any other single factor.

Paul Hawken

Here we go. The previous chapters helped us accept and single out the tools of improvisation. Look at them more closely. Wear them around a bit. Like any other skill, we learned the scales, ran the trials, and built up a few calluses. We needed the time to separate out the behaviors, dissect them to further our understanding. At some point however, we need to jump in and play the game, sing the song, or fill the entire canvas. Now's the time.

This section of the book allows you a chance to put it all together. The following pages provide some specific exercises, questions, and scenarios to take a more holistic approach to changing your thinking, your relationships, and your lifestyle. The collection allows you to play, experiment, and become an applied improviser yourself.

Eventually, the behaviors will become second nature. Until then, remind yourself to YES, AND! — ACCEPT reality, BUILD to the greatest potential, and ACT at the highest level.

Put the power in "And!"

1. Find **Focus** — determine what this moment is about
2. Be **In the Moment** — remain awake and aware to seize opportunities
3. Know **Who/What/Where** — adapt to the people, the issues, and the environment
4. Allow **Give and Take** — realize all voices can contribute to a free exchange of ideas
5. Decide and **Commit** — take the risk and take action

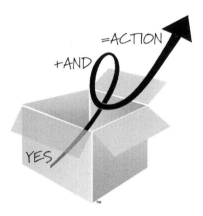

The exercises are organized into four sections:

- Teambuilding/Conflict Resolution
- Leadership
- Communication
- Innovation

The challenges seem to typically fall into these four buckets. Each section allows you to practice all the tools either individually or in tandem.

One final reminder: To improvise your way through life is an ongoing pursuit. You will have fun at times with these exercises and at other times be frustrated.

Try them more than once. Because everything is different from before at any given moment, including yourself, you will learn new things each time. Morph them so they are more useful to you. Keep a journal. Take time to reflect. Share your observations with others. Keep at it and then invent your own.

Teambuilding/Conflict Resolution: Exploration and Application

We've all experienced good and bad teamwork. We've had our fair share of conflict. Use the following exercises to have the conversations you need to have, strengthen the team, and just have fun.

1. Envision Positive Results

Use Yes, And! to strengthen collaboration, build energy, and enable results.

Part One: Use the first two columns in the grid below to help you identify the many ways you can Yes, And! the people around you. Use the third column to help you envision the positive results.

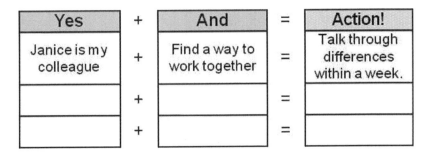

Yes	+	And	=	Action!
Accept	+	Build	=	Act
	+		=	
	+		=	

Part Two: Use each column to apply Yes, And! to a specific situation, issue, and/or individual.

Yes	+	And	=	Action!
Janice is my colleague	+	Find a way to work together	=	Talk through differences within a week.
	+		=	
	+		=	

Think about:

- In what ways am I saying "No but..." rather than "Yes, And!"?
- Am I resistant to new ideas or approaches? How does that affect others?
- Am I someone to whom others come to share ideas?
- Do I ask for help when I need to?
- Am I okay with others getting the credit for my ideas or my work?
- Do I do what I say I will do?

2. Make Each Other Look Great

Improvisation requires we tell each other the truth. The intention is that by telling the truth we make each other look great. We discover our strengths, we find ways to improve, we make bold choices, and we find ourselves.

If I can trust you to tell me the truth to my face, I trust you. If I trust you to have my back, I can do anything. And so can you.

Make a list of the types of people you interact with regularly, i.e. customer, team member. Next, identify one way to make each of them look great.

People I interact with	Ways to make them look great
Janice	Give her credit for her idea in our staff meeting

3. Preserve patterns that work

We can't and don't want to change everything at once. That's chaotic and costly. Each small shift in direction, like the tiller on a sailboat, can slow you down. So, we need to be thoughtful and intentional about the change. To do that, start by making a list of what's working. It can be a process, a relationship, or a means of communication.

After you create the list, in the right hand column, highlight the reasons each thing is working.

What's working?	Why is it working?

4. Roadblocks to Change

We're good at putting up roadblocks. We throw them in our own path. We also litter the path for others. Let's face it, most of us, unless it's our idea, don't like change. Because of that, we suffer.

Here's the nicest little summary of suffering I've ever found. It's called "The Four Causes of Suffering."[14]

- We don't get what we want
- We get it and we don't like it
- We have to endure the absence of those we love
- Or the presence of those we don't

Obviously, we won't avoid suffering altogether. We shouldn't. Suffering generates powerful creativity. Note Edward Munch's *The Scream*. At work however, it helps to be more objective about what needs to change. We can moan and groan for a bit and then, it's time to accept what isn't working. We won't always get our way so, let's accept reality and get on with it.

Take a look at what's getting in your way. What are the obstacles preventing you from being as efficient, consistent, and communicative as you can be? Be honest and make your lists. Think about why it's not working on your own at first. Then, engage the rest of the team and get their perspective.

---

[14]   Huber, Cheri. Adapted from: *How You Do Anything Is How You Do Everything: A Workbook*. 1988. Keep It Simple Books.

What's not working?	Why isn't it working?

Now, what are you going to do about it?

What will change?	How will it change?

5. Travel Light

If you're going to get moving, you can't take everything or do everything. You'll have to prioritize.

Pause first though. You may find that you're the reason you're overwhelmed. You're hanging on to things you don't really need to do. If you're honest, they may even be things you're doing for the wrong reasons. Perhaps it is one of these reasons:

- No one else will do it as well as I do
- I want the credit — it might get me a raise or promotion
- I want to cover my butt
- I'm doing it so I don't have to do something else

Use the chart to help you identify what to keep and what to let go.

Must Keep	Let Go

6. Peek Behind the Curtain

Next time you go to a theater, think about what went on backstage before the show. How many hours did they practice? Who tested the sound system? How many times did they rerun the scenes? How many hours did performers spend memorizing lines? Who checked to make sure every seat in the house could see and hear the action? We know when it's done poorly. Next time you marvel at a performance, take time to pay attention to what made the show a success.

Try this at work, too. Next time you hear a great presentation or watch a leader masterfully manage conflict or notice how effortlessly a team accomplished a goal, take time to go backstage.

Invite the individual or team members out for a cup of coffee. Ask them to dissect the process for you. How did they prepare for the talk? What were the thinking processes and action steps that led to the resolution? How did they get to kumbaya? How did the team start out? How well did they know each other? What did they do to create the comfort level? How did they divide roles and responsibilities? What were the expectations? What made them successful?

7. Stop Meeting So Much

If you can avoid a meeting, don't have one. If you can't avoid a meeting, then have one for the right reasons. Have a meeting only if you actually need people to be together to brainstorm, dialogue and/or make a decision.

Next, Yes, And! what makes meetings productive.

A. Find your focus before you meet:

- Know why you're meeting
- Know what you're meeting about
- Know how much time you need
- Know what's next

B. Use Who/What/Where:

- Invite only the people who need to be there
- Stick to six: More than six and people become passive. Less than six means less energy and ideas.
- Send participants an agenda ahead of time

C. During the meeting — Be in the moment:

- Set the ground rules of Yes, And!
- Create the right environment
  - Comfortable sensory space that can be messy and kinesthetic
  - Playful atmosphere — food, games, toys
- Clarify the focus
- Stay in the moment
- Facilitate give and take
- Commit to action with deadlines and assignments

D. At the end of the meeting — Commit:

- Summarize the results and decisions
- Agree on the next steps
- Be accountable
- Follow up on agreements
- Critique the meeting for continuous improvement

8. Get a Life

Start by broadening your universe. Read the sports page if you hate sports. Go to a museum. Walk the dog on a new route. Observe.

Read the comics. Go to a new bar. Eat something you've never tasted before. Allow your senses to come alive.

In my stress workshop, one of the exercises I use invites participants to peel an orange. It's something they've done many times. So many that, for most, it's second nature. That's what we're trying to overcome.

We begin in silence. They close their eyes and just hold the orange. Slowly, they begin to peel it. I have them pause and smell the peel. They fold it and release the mist. The peeling continues at a slow pace to heighten awareness, to engage all the senses. By the time they finally eat a slice, their shoulders have relaxed and their faces look peaceful.

Next time you're feeling overwhelmed, remember the orange. Take a break from hurriedly ingesting a energy bar on the way to the next meeting and give yourself permission to slow down and live in the present moment.

The more you allow your senses to come alive, the more alive you become.

9. Simplify

Artists give us the gift of simplifying our complex world. Most visual artists, unless they are super-realists, take out everything

> **"Our words** must seem to be inevitable."
> W.B. Yeats

they don't need and suggest the rest. A slash of white paint becomes a sail. Wet pigment on wet paper suggests the sky. A flick of a pallet knife suggests a branch.

Leave out what you don't need in your message, your design, or your process. Get back to only what's necessary and leave the rest behind.

10. Use Analogies

Here are a few to get you started. Then try some of your own.

Message	Simile or Metaphor
Your actions affect others.	For gears to turn, the notches have to line up just right. If one wheel doesn't turn, they all stop. If your efforts don't move the wheel, stop.
Have a vision and get us there.	To plan a trip: know the destination, mode of transportation, the route, and schedule. Now we know how to pack.
To be agile and profitable, spend less.	For your body to be healthy, you need to lower your cholesterol. More exercise gives you more energy.
Tell the truth.	Start with your dog. Stop saying, "I'll be right back."
Skill building: allow time/failure.	Learning to ride a bike: how much time? How much skin did you leave on the pavement?

11. Give Gifts

Don't wait for the holidays to give gifts. Holidays are too infrequent and expensive. See the gifts around you and give them away...often. Accept gifts when they're offered.

Share positive feedback. Don't hoard your praise or wait for the right moment. Tell your fellow player, your employee, your spouse, or the tollbooth operator that you're grateful for him or her. Look for things that are working and say so.

Don't be disingenuous, but don't be miserly either. People need to hear how smart they are, how hard they made you laugh, what a calming influence they have on the team, or how their energy motivated the rest of the group. Do it now.

12. Receive Gifts

Receiving is harder for us. When someone praises us, we're inclined to play down our efforts, point to someone more "worthy," or deny the words altogether. We need to say, "Thank you." When we don't, we're saying to the other person, "You're wrong." That's offensive don't you think? We can share the accolades but we shouldn't start out by negating them.

Constructive feedback is also a gift. Getting it, however, requires us to ensure the other people feel safe enough to give it. We need to let them know that we're not going to take it personally, talk badly about them, or take them off the committee. To get constructive feedback, let others know you want it. Not just through your words but your tone and posture. Make it easy for them. Ask specific questions. Then, listen. Don't talk through them. Don't get defensive. Don't explain. Just listen. You don't have to take the advice, but if you ask for it, let them tell you.

13. Collaborate

Don't just get people in the same room. Take the time to build a team. Be intentional about who you invite, how you structure the interaction, and take the time to build relationships.

This is especially important if you're task-oriented. You may assume that because people know what needs to be done, they'll trust each other enough to share the right information to get it done. Wrong. Teamwork or collaboration doesn't just happen.

Make time to cultivate the culture and do it right. Putting in the time at the beginning reaps great rewards in the end. Skipping this step, or skimping on the investment, dramatically diminishes the return.

For example:

- Be sure people know why they're on the team
- Clarify the purpose of the team
- Avoid coercing participation — if they don't want to be there, they'll drag the others down
- Have them set the ground rules and post them
- Allow time for fun and laughter
- Deal with conflict when it happens

14. Resolve Conflict

Be realistic about conflict. Yes, And! the fact that none of us like it. That we think if we get involved in conflict, we're not nice people. Thinking that way encourages harmony at the cost of telling the truth. It just delays the necessary conversations and makes it worse.

Actually, addressing conflict shows respect. It demonstrates that you care what the other person thinks, you value the relationship, and that you're willing to be uncomfortable toward a greater end. Add to that, the more quickly conflict is resolved, the sooner we all get back to the business of business: productivity and profit. Reduced conflict means improved morale and greater retention. Reduced conflict means improved customer service. Reduced conflict means greater teamwork, less stress, and increased innovation. Besides, it's just a lot more fun when people aren't fighting.

Leaders accept that conflict is inevitable. It's a natural part of living and working together. It causes us to make the changes we've been avoiding and opens door to new opportunities. In fact, the absence of conflict reveals the absence of trust.

It won't unfortunately take care of itself. We need to initiate action and understand that conflict can't always be resolved. If we focus more on making people happy rather than inviting dialogue however, we may accept inadequate resolution leading ultimately to deeper disagreements.

Journal Exercises

1. List some key causes of stress in your life. Decide to focus on ONE of those this week. Identify how you will manage the stress and record your insights.
2. Record how you used one of the techniques of handling conflict to modify your behavior and resolve the issue.

Leadership: Exploration and Application

Leadership is risky business. You know that. Whether you serve on a neighborhood board, hold a position in a company, or are a parent, you have others watching you. Pretending you're perfect can put a lot of strain on you and be discouraging for those around you.

If you were the perfect leader, why would anyone else even try? The intent here is obviously to strengthen your leadership skills. The paradox is that they'll work best if you're honest, vulnerable, and surround yourself with others who care about you and are willing to provide honest feedback.

1. Find Your Light

Great performers, like great leaders, find their light. They don't wait for the tech crew to find them on stage. They seek out the light and step in.

> **"The best companies** distinguish themselves from all others by their ability to adapt to and capitalize on a rapidly changing, often unpredictable environment."
> *Organization Dynamics Magazine*

Amateur performers forget this. Consumed with how they look on stage, they freeze or overact. They wait to be "invited" into a scene. They worry about being liked by the audience rather than giving them what they came for, what they need.

The same is true of new leaders. They seek to please rather than lead. They are tentative rather than bold. They live at the edge of the light instead of stepping boldly into their role.

Great leaders courageously step out and step up. They Yes, And! their strengths, their teams, and the challenge before them. They acknowledge weaknesses and build strong teams to fill in the gaps. They invite genius or they provide team members with the training to make them so. They take inventory of their resources and find a way to get more of what they need. They observe, listen, and then act. They encourage others to step up as well.

On stage, the action provides the wild inventiveness that brings us such great entertainment. Players don't wait around for something better. They work with what they have and build on it.

Take inventory of your own actions. Are you finding your light or waiting for someone to shine it on you? Are you initiating and contributing? Do you wait for the perfect opportunity to come your way?

2. Share the Stage

Bill Murray, that philosopher king who doubles as a comedian, said that improvisation is "the most important group work since they built the pyramids." He's right. Great groups accomplish great things. They accomplish those "big, hairy, audacious goals."

The analogy of the pyramids is a good one. They're huge. They're in the middle of a hot desert. Somehow someone got a bunch of people to go to the desert and schlep around heavy rocks.

Amazing. We have trouble getting people to be pleasant on the phone.

So how do we get employees or our kids committed enough to do the impossible? We start by getting them to see the pyramid. We then get everyone to say, "Great idea. Let's do it." It becomes their idea, not just yours. To try it:

- Slow down to see the needs, the people, the opportunities
- Be sure you know how it benefits others
- State your vision in ways others can see it too
- Be bold and try it

3. Use Active Moments to Discover Your Story

Often great leader stories come from active moments. Active moments provide a roadmap to helping us understand who we are. Active moments shape us.

> **"Chance favors**
> the prepared mind."
> *Louis Pasteur*

What is an active moment? Think of a moment in time after which everything was completely different. You were, are, no longer the same because of that event. Your life took a dramatic turn because of this specific incident.

Looking for patterns among the active moments can provide us with insight into who we are as a leader and can present us with a guide for developing our vision. Noticing the patterns of the moments we choose and how we react to them are good ways to reveal who you really are.

4. Hire the Right Person

Yes, And! is also about believing what is right before your eyes. It's not about believing what you want to be true or even need to be true. It's about believing what is true.

The next time you interview candidates, pay attention. Avoid the trap of envisioning who you want them to be. How they fit into your agenda. How they might make you look. Stop trying to make them into someone you wish they were.

When people show you who they are, believe them.

5. Stop Trying to Get It Right

Following a scene in one of my workshops, the student looked at me and said, "I know that was painful to watch." I was surprised and said, "Why did you think that?"

"It was painful to do, so I'm sure it was painful to watch."

Her comment made me sad. She was worried about what I was thinking. Instead of focusing on the scene, she focused on me, on what I thought. She wanted to "do it right." She wanted to please me. Blame traditional schooling for this if you like. Teachers taught us that if we got it right, we got an "A." If we behaved a certain way, we went out for recess. If we were quiet in class, they liked us.

Unfortunately, corporations have fallen in the same trap. We call it, "pay for performance." These models, in school and in the workplace, reduce risk. They squelch creativity. They assume there is only one right answer.

Today, let go of trying to be right and allow yourself to be real.

6. Learn From A German

Although some tried too hard to "get it right" in my workshops, others enlightened themselves and the rest of us by taking a risk. We take notice when people step out and take risks. Fraulein Gert showed me this. She taught German at a nearby college and decided she needed to loosen up a bit. She wanted to perk up her teaching style so she signed up for a one-day intensive workshop. Her tall stature and serious expression made her instantly intimidating.

After warm ups, she volunteered immediately for a scene. Her bold choices impressed all of us. She built a sand castle in an imaginary sandbox, earnestly applied lipstick on her way to the make-believe prom, cooed at a lion in our fantasy zoo, and even wept at the chair-now-casket over the death of a stranger.

All of this happened in an empty meeting room in the middle of the day. She didn't care what we thought of her. Because she believed in the scene, we did too.

When we broke for lunch, she broke character and continued to exhibit Yes, And! She remained in the moment and generously invested in the other class members. She listened as another participant talked about what it's like to be bipolar and why he was expelled from school in his senior year.

She gave gifts and took risks. She focused on the other person rather than herself. She was confident enough to praise others, gentle enough to hear pain, and direct enough to tell the truth.

Today, take inspiration from her story and try it yourself:

- Stop playing it safe and be bold
- Tell the truth to one person and expect it back
- Share a "crazy" idea and be proud of it
- Seize the moment

7. Build Your Brand

We build our brand either by default or intention. Regardless of how we approach or don't approach it, we all have a brand. Each of us behaves, dresses, and communicates in a way that, unless we're schizophrenic, consistently underscores who we are. To help you become intentional with your brand, try the following:

- Have five people you trust describe you as if they were talking to someone you never met.
- Look and listen for patterns. When you walk into a room, how do people typically respond? Smiles? Questions? Ignore you?

- Observe how others are treated when they walk into the room. What is the difference and why?

8. Play the Lead

Athletes suit up for the game. Actors put on a costume. Ninjas don their shells. They get ready. How they dress, what they wear is a big part of that.

Whether you like it or not, what you wear says a lot about you as a leader. How you dress affects how you carry yourself. It strengthens or weakens your confidence level. It isn't your whole brand but it certainly contributes to the overall impression.

Start by dressing well. Obviously, this means different things to different people. How you dress needs to fit what you do. No matter how Bohemian you feel, you do have to be sensitive to how others perceive you and dress accordingly.

Even better, find your brand. Be true to who you are and what you want to accomplish. This helps you make the decision from the inside out. You'll be more comfortable and communicate the truth about you.

9. Hire the Best

It isn't elitist to want to be the best and hire the best. When we hire people, we want them to be better at the stuff we're hiring them for than we are. That's simple. Why would you hire someone who is only as good as you are?

Think about your gaps. Your challenges. Your Achilles heel. Rather than turn a blind eye to your faults or try to hide them, expose yourself. (You know what I mean.)

Get a coach or a trusted confidant and ask them to be brutally honest. Providing clear, direct, truthful feedback is one of the kindest things we can do for each other. Once you have the information, amass a team that will make everyone better.

10. Your Voice

The way you speak has a lot to do with how people perceive you as a leader. The more relaxed you are, the more relaxed your vocal chords. Relaxed vocal chords help you speak more naturally. More conversationally.

When we're stressed, we sound whiny. We're irritating. That's a sure way to clear the room or be ignored.

To avoid this, find ways throughout the day to "warm up." Hum on the way to a meeting. Find vocal exercises that you enjoy. Practice tongue twisters. Sigh. Sing with the radio.

Surprisingly, this translates into accessibility. The more relaxed you sound, the more comfortable you are in your own skin, the more likely you are to take your focus off of yourself. You can more easily focus on the person(s) in front of you.

11. Discover What Makes This Day Different

I've mentioned that at *The Second City*, we wrote the shows. We would take the stuff of daily life — the traffic ticket, the panhandler needing another dollar, the broken eggs in our grocery bag — and write a scene. Obviously, just by being alive, we had plenty of material.

The question we asked ourselves, to create thoughtful entertainment from these mundane experiences, was: "What makes this day different?" We'd gotten speeding tickets before, handed the homeless some change, or grumbled about a bum bagger. This time, however, something, everything was different. This time, a different decision, colliding events, or emotional perspective changed everything. This is the stuff that we want to see on the stage. We come to watch someone do something bold and different than we typically do everyday.

You have the same opportunity. Each day, you have the chance to make the day different — whether it's to speak up about an injustice, inject energy into the weekly staff meeting, or engage that shy person on your team.

Each of us has the chance, every day, to make the world a better place.

Believe that not sharing your talents, insights, or time would be an act of outright negligence. Believe you would do a disservice to the world if you didn't share your perspective, stop to say a kind word, or get that product to market.

12. Shed Your Skin, Wear Another

Some professional actors actually choose footwear that fits the character they intend to portray. They say it helps them "walk around in the character's skin."

> **"Seek to understand** before being understood."
> *Stephen Covey*

As a leader, you're trying to do the same thing. Shed your skin. Get out of your own world. Walk around in another. Basically, build empathy.

Next time you attend a meeting, look at the shoes in the room. How are they different from yours? Figuratively, or literally, step into another pair and note the difference in your behavior and theirs when you interact with them.

13. Skip the Stress

Harry Mills, Ph.D. a licensed psychologist in Florida has one of my favorite definitions of stress. He describes stress as "The... anticipation of our inability to respond adequately to a perceived demand from our physical or social environment, accompanied by our anticipation of negative consequences for our expected inadequate response." In other words, we get what we expect.

To help you manage stress, try listing something that typically stresses you out. Take a second look at what you wrote and identify five different ways you could change it into an opportunity. Yes, And! to see what you can discover.

Something I stress about	How I harness the hassle
Computer seizes up	1. Rearrange meeting times so they occur while IT works on my computer
	2. Get that new computer I had my eye on
	3. Find a new way to complete the task (i.e. don't use PowerPoint)
	4. Take a 15 minute nap
	5. Seize the chance to get to know the computer technician a little better

14. Sure. Why Not?

Say "yes" to the very next idea you hear. No matter what it is or who suggested it, try saying to yourself, "Sure, I'll listen ...why not?" Then:

- Find at least one thing you can agree with
- Add to it
- Enjoy the ride

15. Status and Power

Just like we all have a brand whether we realize it or not, we communicate our status and power level to others whether we are cognizant of it or not. We tend to default, be comfortable with, one or the other. Status and power do not necessarily reflect title, gender, age, or position, although they may be and studies do show some patterns. What's important to you is to know what others' experience.

Use the examples to observe this behavior. Check your observations with others. You'll find that typically, people of the same culture interpret these in similar ways. Across cultures, perceptions may vary widely.

Awareness of status and power allows you to address behavior in yourself or others that either helps or hinders communication.

Behavior	Low Status	High Status
Verbal pacing	Fast. Speaks too quickly, interrupts themselves often.	Slow. Comfortable with pauses, chooses words carefully.
Vocal timber	Voice sounds pinched, too high, vocal chords sound stressed.	Open, natural quality. Easy to listen to.
Volume	Speaks too softly. Sentences trail off at the end.	Appropriate volume for the environment and number of people.
Movement	Fast. Jittery. Moves around a lot.	Relaxed. Moves when necessary. Physicality complements message
Eye Contact	Does not maintain eye contact. Breaks gaze often.	Looks at people. Sees them and listens intently.
Space	Does not occupy space. Hands under the table. Poor posture. Keeps their distance.	Takes ownership of the space. Takes up space. Good posture. Comfortable proximity to others.
Interaction	Does not initiate. Waits to be invited into the conversation.	Speaks up. Appropriate level of give and take.
Elevation	Stays seated. Lowers head. Slumping posture.	Stands. Perches on desk. Good posture.
Language	Asks questions. Qualifies with "I think" or the equivalent.	Uses statements and assertions.
Facial Expressions	Closed. Low affect. Reactive.	Open. Comfortable. Initiates. Intentional and relaxed.

16. Yes, And! the Obvious

When others don't meet our expectations we get frustrated. We blame them. But, when is the last time you openly stated your expectations? If you haven't, now is a good time. Here are some examples:

- I expect you all to treat each other with respect by making each other look great
- I expect you to take initiative when you discover a way to do something better
- I expect you to come to work every day and function as if you owned the company...because you do
- I expect you to be able to articulate who we are and how we make the world a better place

Journal Exercises

1. Push your status to either higher or lower than is typical for you. What changes did you notice in yourself? How have reactions from others varied from previous experience?
2. Read a biography of a famous leader who made the kind of impact you would like to make. How might this person's perspective change your decisions for the long-term?
3. Use social media to follow someone who leads very differently than you do. What can you learn from his or her choices?

Communication: Exploration and Application

Improving communication is a lifelong pursuit. Knowing this probably either frustrates you or entices you. Since none of us is going to get this right all of the time, start by giving yourself a break. Have fun with these.

1. Hit the Ball

Unless you're living on some mountaintop somewhere, you, like everyone else, are overwhelmed with...well, everything — meetings, to-do lists, appointments, errands, projects, politics. Whatever it is, there's too much of it and it's coming at you all at once.

The same has been happening to your audience all day. By the time they see you, most of them are spinning. If you're not careful about how you add to their level of overstimulation, you're likely to confuse them, bore them, or put them to sleep.

To capture their interest and get them to act, your message must be simple, focused, and memorable. Marketers are great at this. Television advertisements are some of the best examples around. In 30, sometimes even as little as 15 seconds, they serve up a mini-meal that matches the taste buds of their particular audience. In the good ones, the messages are quick, entertaining, and unforgettable.

How do they do it? They've identified the one thing their audience needs to know and why. You can, and should do the same. Start by ensuring you know your audience. (See audience-mapping exercise later in this section.)

Then, identify the one thing they need to know and why. Capture this in one sentence. It's tempting to allow yourself to get flabby here by using more than one sentence. Think of the bull's-eye of a target. Try to be that specific.

Use the following guidelines to "hit the ball." (Refer to the chapter on focus for more tips.)

a. Make a statement
b. Be concrete
c. Limit your focus
d. Be inclusive — what do they have in common and why should they care
e. Have a point of view

Raise the stakes: Try picking the one person or group that intimidates you the most. Perhaps it's your most difficult client, your crabby neighbor, or your mother-in-law. Success with the toughest client will give you the confidence for success with others.

2. Avoid Distractions

It's never taken much to distract ourselves or another person. With all the technology at our fingertips, it's even easier now. That would be great if distractions improved communication. It would be fabulous if it deepened our relationships. Because it doesn't, we need to tame the beast. We need to consciously reduce our distractions.

To start, identify what, for you, are the real temptations. Is it your computer monitor? A window? That shiny object on your desk? If so, next time you're on the phone, try this:

- Turn your back on your monitor
- Close the blinds
- Close your eyes

3. Audience Mapping

    a.   In four minutes, using a pad of sticky notes, write down one trait that your audience members have in common per sheet. Obviously not every individual will share the descriptor but it fits most of the people in attendance. Push yourself and try to write at least 20. (See examples below.)

    b.   Choose the top three characteristics that will affect their response to your message.

    c.   Use these observations to help shape the way you structure content. This will help you more effectively choose which stories you tell, how much data to include, and the visuals to include.

3. One, Two, Three (Rule of Threes)

Jokes, stories, and sermons typically are structured in threes. In geometry, the triangle is the strongest. Research indicates that our brains respond most positively to this structure. Suffice it to say here, that three creates strong, relatable, memorable constructs.

For your messaging, once you've found the one thing you want your audience to know, divide the concept into three major points. Can you use five or seven? Sure. But, for simplicity, try three for starters.

4. Objection: Sustained

Because most people object to new ideas before they've even heard them, you need to get to the objection before they do. Having the conversation before you actually talk to the other person helps a lot. Here's your chance to be a playwright.

1. Follow the instructions above for shaping your message.
2. List at least five potential, reasonable objections to accepting your idea.
3. In dialogue format, write out the conversation in at least two ways:
   a. How you hope it transpires
   b. As if it went terribly wrong

5. 80 Percent of You Told Me So

We communicate volumes through eye contact and body language. Some statisticians suggest, as much of 80 percent of communication is nonverbal. If that's true, much of what you say doesn't matter. How you say it, matters immensely.

Use the following exercise from Viola Spolin's *Improvisation for the Theater*, to improve your awareness of the affect nonverbal communication has on the transference of information.

Players assign an emotion to a specific facial feature, for example: an annoyed chin, a frustrated nose, or ecstatic eyebrows.

1. On individual cards list a state of being. Examples include: confused, frightened, ecstatic.
2. On another set of cards list facial features. Examples include: eyebrows, cheeks, lips.
3. Each player should take one card from each set. For example, you may end up with: confused cheeks.
4. Now have a conversation while at the same time trying to communicate confusion with your cheeks. Talk about anything, but as much as possible, have a genuine conversation.

Note: To start, you may want to do this the first time with people you know well. Certainly, you'll laugh. You will also gain insights into how facial expression affects your message.

Try this several times and vary your tone, facial features, and/or your posture. Discuss the impact on the message and why. Try it with a contentious topic. Discuss how your nonverbal behavior invites dissention or agreement.

7. Famous Mistakes

Collect stories of famous leaders who've made mistakes. You should have no trouble finding plenty.

Write each story on a slip of paper. Have team members choose a story from a hat and read it aloud to the group. Accept the consequences of the mistake. Now, brainstorm how that mistake can be positive. How might you "spin" it to look like a success? What can you learn from this?

Next, have someone share one of his or her recent "mistakes." Again, brainstorm all the ways this can be positive for the company. What insights can you gain from the future for this?

8. Same Page

Have two volunteers sit next to each other on chairs. They will take questions from the rest of the group. They must answer each question in unison...same word at the same time.

Afterward, talk about what they did to be successful. What presented difficulty? How could it be even more successful?

The game is fun. It's also obviously artificial. How can playing the game help you get alignment with your message?

9. Attitude Walk

You can do this exercise alone or with others. Choose one of the expressions below and, while you're moving about, repeat the word or phrase to yourself. Say it in your head. Don't think about the meaning; just repeat the actual word(s.) Note how your posture, gait, and facial expression change as you do.

Happy	Call me	Fear	Dislike
Sad	Be quiet	Disbelief	I like you
Angry	I don't know	Disgust	Interest
Disinterest	Boredom	I'm late	I'm sorry
Anticipation	Money	Confidence	Impatience

After playing, consider what words/phrases you can repeat to make your contributions more positive and impactful to others.

10. Don't Be Tone-deaf

If it's true that what you say to yourself changes the message, it's certainly true that what you say and how you say it changes the message. This isn't news to you. But, because we get busy, we don't pay attention to our tone as much as we should. We become tone-deaf in our drive to meet a deadline, get the promotion, or make the sale.

To experience it yourself, experiment with three tones that will mean different things as you say the following:

- A person's name
- Really
- Sure

11. Think on Your Feet

- In your next encounter with another person, focus on hearing the person who is speaking to you and make eye contact.
- Avoid planning your response as you listen.
- Avoid creating an answer to what they are saying.
- Observe. Listen.
- Pause. Now respond in the most genuine way possible.

12. Language Matters

Stand-up comedians may lull us into thinking that they thought up that brilliant retort on the spot. It just came to them. In fact, the greatest comedians labor over each word in a stand-up routine.

Here's how a Marx Brothers publicist, Teet Carle, remembered the way Groucho Marx prepared his routines from the book *Groucho*.

"...Groucho pored over a single word, trying different candidates for a punch line... Preparing to examine his patient, Dr. Hackenbush washes up. He removes his watch, glances suspiciously at Rumann, and then tosses it into a basin of water: 'I'd rather have it rusty than missing.' On the tour, Carle wrote, 'Gone and disappear were each used forty-four times; missing got fifty voicings. Every time, the latter word brought the biggest laugh.' In another sketch Chico tries to sell Groucho a discounted book: 'One dollar and you remember me all your life.' Groucho: 'That's the most nauseating proposition I ever had.' Adds Carle: 'Among other words tried out were obnoxious, revolting, disgusting, offensive, repulsive, disagreeable, and distasteful. The last two of these words never got more than titters. The others elicited various degrees of ha-has. But nauseating drew the roars. I asked Groucho why that was so.

'I don't know. I really don't care. I only know the audiences told us it was funny.'"[15]

Next time you prepare a presentation, take some time to "road test" the language before you use it.

13. Values Cards Pictionary

We make assumptions that the words we use everyday mean the same thing to the people around us. Obviously, this causes at best, confusion, and at worse, conflict.

When you have to visualize an abstract concept like a value, suddenly you find yourself simplifying the idea and using symbols to communicate. The symbols you choose, consciously and unconsciously, allow you to make those concepts more concrete.

For this exercise, set up the space just as you would for Pictionary® using the same rules and timing constraints. Once you've played, use the drawings, conversations, and shouted guesses to talk about values. What surprised you? Were there any the group just couldn't guess? What are the differences in perception?

Materials:

- Cards — each listing a particular value (*The Leadership Challenge* by Kouzes and Posner[16] offers a nice set or make your own. Examples include honesty, freedom, service etc.)
- Timer
- Easel or white board
- Markers

---

[15]   Kanfer, Stefan. *Groucho: The Life and Times of Julius Henry Marx*. 2000. New York: Alfred A. Knopf, pp. 211-212.

[16]   Kouzes, James and Barry Z. Posner. *The Leadership Challenge. 2008. Jossey-Bass.*

14. Red Ball, Green Ball

Earlier in the book, we noted that assumptions can create connections. They invite others in.

Sometimes, however, if we're not careful, we act on incorrect assumptions. Since perception affects decision-making, relationships, and productivity, it's important to take time to be sure everyone has the same understanding. This exercise invites you to explore unconscious understanding of processes, terminology, or expectations.

Find three foam balls each of a different color. For example, red, green, and yellow.

Here's how to play: One person starts with all three balls. She holds up the green ball and says to the group, "I have a red ball here. I will throw it to one of you and say, 'Red ball.'" As you catch it, you say, "Red ball." Continue to throw the ball randomly back and forth for about two minutes. Stop the play and introduce the next ball by holding up the red ball and saying, "green ball." Continue the play and then add the yellow ball calling it a different color, like blue ball, until participants are throwing and catching all three balls.

Once you stop the play, say the color given to the ball, and ask someone to set it down in the middle of the circle.

Use the following questions to reflect on the experience.

1. What did you experience through this exercise?
2. Why didn't anyone correct me if they saw the ball as a different color?
3. What in our culture might you be perceiving differently than other teammates, industry standards, or our customers. Consider terminology, projects, roles, and responsibilities etc.

Journal Exercises

1. Record times when you lose focus. What does it take to regain focus? Describe the difficulties and record strategies for improving focus.

2. Tune in to your favorite late-night talk show host. You want to catch the first few minutes of the monologue. Notice the first words out of his or her mouth. If you have time, watch the entire monologue and note the flow. Did the host use the rule of threes? How did the monologue end? How can you apply this to your next presentation?

Innovation: Exploration and Application

We equate originality with innovation. Earlier in the book we observed that the best way to ensure you're original is to be yourself. The more relaxed you are, the more in the moment, the more playful, the more likely you will see the world in the most unique way possible: your way.

1. Be Grateful

Sometimes it's important just to be grateful for what you have. Think of the last time you said thank you to someone who dared to speak up and make a suggestion. Instead of hanging back and playing it safe, they did something. They stirred the pot. They acted like a catalyst.

We need to remember how hard it is to make that first move. It's time we see this kind of courage as a gift and stop to say thank you. Thanks for getting us moving. Thanks for giving us something to play with. Thanks for having the "chutzpah" to find your light.

2. Be Intentional

Take a good long look at a typical day. Consider the assumptions you make — how long it will take you to shower, get to work, eat lunch.

Consider how much time you've allotted for the "small talk" the amount of time the people you see each day might need. You might as well admit that, since nothing goes as planned, it's hubris to act as if it will.

Start your day as if you expect to be interrupted. Expect people to show up at your door, give you a call, drop a box on your foot.

After doing this for a few days, note behavior changes when others interrupt you. How has your overall mood changed? Are you responding differently than you might have if you hadn't planned for it? What new insights does this give you about the challenges you face and the people you work with?

> **"Improvisation is a disciplined** craft. Its skills can be learned…and applied to any situation. As a team-based rather than an individual-based technique, improvisation offers a different method of approaching problems or challenges."
> *Organizational Dynamics Magazine*

3. Wake Up

Observe. Notice the way people walk. Listen to the words they use. Pay attention to the color of the room, the weather, the sound of the air conditioner when it kicks on.

Keep a log of these little moments for two weeks. Then, review your notes and look for patterns. What insights does this heightened awareness give you about the people around you, your products, your customers, and need in the marketplace? Mine these moments for great ideas. Keep your knees bent, your eyes open, and your options flexible.

4. Go to a Show

You may have experienced a lot of entertainment tagged as improvisation. These shows, along with local improvisation troupes, have done a great job of entertaining us. We've shared a lot of laughs thanks to Mike Myers, Steve Carell, Tina Fey, and many, many others.

Observing skilled improvisers is a great way to learn. Go to a show and watch how the players interact on stage. Pay attention to how quickly they initiate a character, accept suggestions, and build to find the scene.

Now think about your business. How could your ability to do the same lead to more business, or improve a product launch, or satisfy a customer?

5. Bring Your Beak to Work

Does your company allow for that 15 percent difference? Internally, do you have that level of diversity in your workforce? Do you attract the variety of talent you need? Externally, do you have that level of diversity in your products? Can the consumer identify the difference? The bottom-line question is: "How can we achieve the flexibility, the adaptability that will lead us to a sustainable level of diversity?"

For one thing, make sure everyone gets an equal chance to contribute. Shutting out that conversation is like hiring a great jazz band for your wedding and only allowing the drummer to play. It might be funny at first, but ultimately it's boring. It's boring for the listeners and boring for the band.

The other musicians just sit there. The band can create an amazing sound together, but you stopped them. You are hearing a small sliver of their capability. You're only hearing what you want to hear, not the full rich sound.

You've also robbed the band of motivation. There's no reason to practice. In fact, there's no reason to show up at all.

This is the same reason our companies fall prey to stagnation. People start to realize that no one is using their ideas, listening to their ideas, or even caring what they brought for lunch — unless it is very smelly. And really, this isn't our goal, is it? To get noticed for what stinks?

People desire to get noticed for their brilliance, not their grievances. We show up because we get a paycheck. True. People stay with a company because they can make their mark. People want to make a difference. If they don't or can't, most times, they move on if they can or wreak havoc if they can't.

How can you make sure you do your part to create an environment where everyone flourishes? It's not about whether you like someone. It's about respect. It's about ensuring we capture all the good ideas. It's about finding the 15 percent difference from our competitor so that the company thrives rather than just survives.

6. Cleaner Fish

Have you heard of the cleaner fish at Australia's Great Barrier Reef? They are the dentists of the sea. They have the job of swimming into the mouths of larger fish, even sharks, and "cleaning" them. They slurp up rotten food that might lead to some sort of fishy periodontal disease.

The cleaner fish get the "house specialty" free of charge, and the larger fish improve their dating life. This is cooperation at its best.

Next time you have a particularly daunting challenge, consider inviting the least likely pairings into the room. What kind of symbiotic relationships can you nourish to achieve some of the most innovative solutions?

8. It's Natural

Tina Fey is a brilliant improviser and a shrewd businessperson. During an interview, she said, "I'm always surprised when I meet someone who thinks that sitting and writing

> "Persons appear by entering into relation to other persons."
> *Martin Buber*

is the only way of creating comedy," she told writer Anne Libera.

"It's like meeting someone who thinks in-vitro fertilization is the only way to make a boa baby. You want to say, 'No, there's this whole other way of doing it that's natural and sometimes pleasurable.'"[17]

If this is true, if improvisation is natural and pleasurable, why do we need to be taught to improvise?

It is natural. The problem is we've gotten away from our natural state. Most unfortunately, many of us have not experienced a safe, trusting, and welcoming environment. The default behaviors inherent in improvisation are no longer intrinsic to our relationships. Because of this, we need to learn them...or relearn them.

To start, pay attention to how you interact with the most important people in your life. If you love them, you give them your full attention. You stay in the moment. You Yes, And! them. You think they're brilliant and they think the same of you. You laugh at the same things. You can't wait to tell them about an experience. Your conversations have a natural give and take. You make commitments and stick to them. You'll even spend hours doing things you dislike just to be with them — turning the compost comes to mind.

Somehow, this doesn't translate to our working relationships. We didn't choose them. They have different values, energy levels, and life experiences. They don't laugh at the same things we do. This means we often feel coerced into developing relationships, especially at first. From here, it doesn't take long to develop a bad attitude. Add to that, they heat up yesterday's fish in the microwave. They disagree with our opinion. They don't like our idea as much as their own. The boss cut the budget. You're understaffed. Sometimes you're just tired. Whatever the reason, the relationship doesn't feel natural. It certainly doesn't invite those altruistic natural behaviors inherent to improvisation.

---

[17]   Libera, Anne and Second City, Inc. *The Second City Almanac of Improvisation. 2004.* Northwestern University Press.

To get back to the natural state, you'll need to make some conscious choices. You'll need to get out of your comfort zone.

If you're going to create together, you'll need to have a shift in attitude. You'll need to find ways to Yes, And! your co-workers. You'll need to make your sandbox bigger and invite them in. Or, you'll need to pick up your pail and shovel and move on.

9. Painting in Your Pocket

Find a postcard of a painting you especially like. Museum stores have plenty of these. So does your local bookstore.

Make this painting your companion for the next month. Take it out when you stop for coffee, are waiting for someone, after placing your order at a restaurant, in the bathroom, before bed, whenever.

Just look at it. You're not trying to get any deep meaning out of it, although you may. You're spending time with it, getting to know it like you would a good friend.

You will observe the elements of art certainly: line, shape, color, texture, value, form, and space. Artists use these building blocks to create a two-dimensional piece. Your brain will also register how the artist used the principles of art to organize the work. These principles include unity, harmony, variety, balance, contrast, proportion, pattern, and rhythm.

It's not important for this exercise that you can identify the elements and principles. This is a more organic, holistic approach toward a deeper understanding of how artists, masters at simplifying the complex, do so to communicate, create meaning.

10. You Look Different Upside Down

Betty Edwards gave the world a gift with her book, *Drawing on the Right Side of the Brain.*[18] She took away the excuse that, as a former art teacher, I heard endlessly. Students and adults moaned that they could not draw. They marveled at the talent of others, but, when it came to themselves, proclaimed with certainty that they could never do what others did with a pencil.

The truth is they could. Betty Edwards famously proclaimed that if you can hold a pencil, you could draw. The problem, she said, is that people don't know how to see. Pick up her book from a bookstore. (Yes, it's that good. It's still in print.) Give yourself 20 minutes a day to try her exercises. You'll be amazed at what you can capture on paper. More importantly, you'll learn to see the world in a new way, a real way. And that's what we're really after isn't it?

11. Polly Want a Culture?

I know this pun is obnoxious, but it got your attention didn't it? Read a book on biomimicry. I like the one by Janine M. Benyus, *Biomimicry: Innovation Inspired by Nature*[19] but there are plenty of good ones out there. While you do, give yourself some field experience. Find a strong ecosystem, a bog, wetlands, or mature forest and observe how all the pieces work together. Note the strength in diversity.

Observe your neighborhood, church, and/or workplace. Is there more evidence of a monoculture or a polyculture? If it's a monoculture, what's missing and how does it negatively affect the dreams of the group. If it's a polyculture, observe the tensions but also strengths that might be missing if everyone was the same.

---

[18] Edwards, Betty. *Drawing on the Right Side of the Brain.* 1979. Harper Collins Publishers.
[19] Benyus, Janine M. *Biomimicry: Innovation Inspired By Nature.* 1997, reissued 2002. New York. Harper Perennial.

---

12. Memorize a Poem

In some ways, this is similar to the Painting in Your Pocket exercise. Memorization takes the brain through some interesting stages. At first, it's tedious. It requires lots of repetition, which makes it boring. To help move this first aspect along a little faster, do this in short bursts. Our brain remembers first and last bits of information. If you spend 15 minutes at a time memorizing, you have more "firsts" and "lasts" than you do if you try to do it for two hours.

Once the words become second nature, the poem gets interesting. We can focus on meaning rather than trying to remember the next line. Savor the words. Live with the lines. As with the painting, notice what carrying these words with you does to your appreciation of language, powers of observation, and stress reduction.

There are so many good poems out there, choosing one may be the hardest part. If you can't find one, use the poem from chapter five, "Nothing Gold Can Stay"[20] by Robert Frost, repeated here for convenience.

> Nature's first green is gold,
> Her hardest hue to hold.
> Her early leaf's a flower;
> But only so an hour.
> Then leaf subsides to leaf.
> So Eden sank to grief,
> So dawn goes down to day.
> Nothing gold can stay.

---

[20] Frost, Robert. "Nothing Gold Can Stay."

13. Find Your Way

Julia Cameron in her book *The Artist's Way: A Spiritual Path to Higher Creativity*,[21] includes excellent exercises for, as she says, "... discovering and recovering your creative self."

These are wonderful to do on your own. They're even better if you can find a small group of like-minded creative types and do these together.

14. Take Long Walks without a Walkman

I know the reference is outdated but I like the alliteration. Plus, Apple Inc. has enough publicity don't you think?

At first, you may be uncomfortable with the wind in your ears or that you're being bombarded with ambient sound. The weaning process for some will be harder than others, especially if you're used to such a sound-controlled world. For some, the boredom factor will be most problematic.

Either way, give it time. Eventually your senses will wake back up and delight you with the warble of a crane, the rattling of a tree branch, or the sound of your own breath. Stay with it.

If you need more convincing, check out the article in *Backpacker Magazine*, "Hiking Makes You Smarter."[22] The writer highlights the work of researcher, David Strayer, Ph.D., whose hypothesis includes that "...exposure to nature causes significant, measurable changes to the brain. These changes let you think more clearly, focus more acutely, and perform to your maximum cognitive ability."

---

[21] Cameron, Julia. *The Artist's Way: A Spiritual Path to Higher Creativity*. 2002. Jeremy P. Tarcher/ Putnam.

[22] Kwak-Hefferan, Elisabeth. "Hiking Makes You Smarter." May 2012. *Backpacker Magazine*.

---

15. Mars Attack

If you didn't see the movie, the reference won't make much sense. Before you go any further, rent the movie, and then come back.

If you have seen the movie, you remember that every time someone plays country music, their brains explode. Obviously, this was bad news for the Martians. For you and I, however, this can be a good thing. Exploding your brain might be just the thing you need to see things in a new way.

Find out what it is that is most unsettling, annoying, or confusing to you. Then, immerse yourself in it, at least for awhile. If you didn't get a roaring headache, and I hope you didn't, figure out what you can Yes, And! from the experience. You already knew you had an adverse reaction. Figuring out why and looking at it in a new way may open some pretty interesting doors.

Journal Exercises

1. Innovation often requires we get out of a rut. Ruts aren't all bad especially if you like to cross-country ski, but they can be confining. Try doing something different in your journal. If you're used to writing in your journal, try drawing. If you typically draw, perhaps resort to symbols. Use a pencil instead of a pen or charcoal or a crayon. Pay attention to how different means of communication and different media invite new ways of expression.

2. For years, people of all persuasions kept journals. When you get stuck on your own, enjoy the observations of others. You'll return to yours with fresh energy and insights. Here are a few recommendations to consider, all very different from each other:

a.   *Teaching a Stone to Talk: Expeditions and Encounters* by Annie Dillard — The Pulitzer Prize-winner writer "explores the world of natural facts and human meanings."

b.   *The Book of Alfred Kantor* by Alfred Kantor — Haunting drawings and commentary from his experience in three Nazi detention camps.

c.   *A Writer's Eye: Field Notes and Watercolors* by Paul Horgan — As he says himself, "My main concern was to make a graphic note which later on would not only show me what I saw but would remind me of how I felt when I saw it."

Practice Scenarios

We probably can agree intellectually to this idea from *Organizational Dynamics Magazine:* "The key task for managers is to explore and innovate in chaotic conditions. Essentially, an organization must be flexible enough to adapt, creative enough to innovate, and responsive enough to learn."

The hard part is to BE that flexible, creative, and responsive. In the moment, we typically default to what is familiar and comfortable. We are not intentional enough about stepping out into the chaos to explore and innovate.

Our default behaviors then do not serve us well. Consider the following three scenarios:

Scenario One

It's 5 p.m. and your supplier just called to tell you the shipment of solar panels for your very best customer, Jane Slidell, will not be in today. Confusion with the order means it's stuck somewhere in Tennessee and that office has closed down for the day. You watch out the window as Jane herself rolls up in her Mercedes to inspect the order. What do you do?

Scenario Two

You are reviewing your notes one last time for your presentation at the regional trade show. It's quite an honor to be asked to speak and the president of the board just slipped into the back of the room. Although you were promised the sound system would be working and you tested it yourself in rehearsal, it's clear that your first words to 1,500 salespeople seated in front of you are clearly not being amplified. What do you do?

Scenario Three

You have one chance to pitch a new project that would make your company a star. The CEO of one of your best customers has finally agreed to give you one hour of his time. You're wearing your best suit; you've had a good breakfast (eggs are "brain food" as your mother used to say so you've had two just in case). Unfortunately, just as you arrive, the CEO's receptionist tells you that his plans have changed and, much to his chagrin he says, he needs to reschedule. What do you do?

None of these situations went the way you hoped or expected. It certainly wasn't for lack of planning or preparing. You pride yourself on the processes you've put into place and you don't leave anything to chance. Your strategy sessions mean that you've done what you can to anticipate economic shifts and your business is poised to take advantage of changes in the marketplace.

In other words, you've planned, prepared, practiced, and pretty much have done everything you could do to ensure that your product, your presentation, and your meeting would be flawless. And, predictably, they don't go as planned. So, what do you do?

Those who fail, wail at the unfairness of it. They blame those around them. They may believe they deserve the expected, the planned, the secure. They are outraged that more would be expected of them and frightened they don't know how to respond. It doesn't take long for this kind of response to impact your business. Talented employees, like customers, grow frustrated and move on. They lose their passion and you lose them.

What if you don't just stand there, immobilized, and hope the moment will pass? What if you approach the moment with confidence, humor, finesse? What if you are able to skillfully improvise and make the most of it? What if you surprise yourself and leave with no regrets. What if you flex in the moment and arrive at a solution...you find a way to make it work. Instead of replaying the moment, over and over while you brushed your teeth, wishing you'd said just the right thing, you leave with a smile on your face. What if you harvest that moment to the fullest and walk away without regret. What if?

Ample hubris leads us to believe we can get the moment back or change the outcome. We'll get another chance, we say to ourselves.

As a leader, later is not a luxury you can afford. You cannot assume that you will have the same opportunity later — to recognize the good job, to thank the employee for taking a risk, to even just take a moment to see the other person for who they are (even if it doesn't serve your purposes). People — employees and clients — are our greatest resource. We can't afford to look past them and take them for granted. We need to make the most of each moment with each of them now. And it has to be just that. A real, genuine moment when you aren't doing something else. Not a divided moment when your attention is in more than one place. Each individual we come in contact with has the right to our full attention in the moment, even if it is short.

In problem scenarios, we're tempted to try to change the circumstances, the processes, or the people. We like to dangle that "if only" around and take a seat with "that'll never happen again." But the unexpected does happen and it will continue to happen. You know that. So, that requires that we get started with the one thing you really can change. You. Wish I had a better answer. If you really do want to solve problems quickly and, well, in the moment, you need to change you.

Whether you acknowledge it or not, you do improvise in the moment and find your way to a solution. At times, the solution is just right. You are insightful, witty, and smooth. Other times, you break out into a sweat, bungle your message, and leave feeling irritated. You are a loser, or so your little inner voice tells you. You say and do all the wrong things on a bad day and, just like Goldilocks, you occasionally hit on behavior that is "just right." Up until now, you thought there wasn't much you could do about it. You told yourself that your uneven performance just meant you lacked the talent those "witty" people seem to have. You figure you are unpredictable. Sometimes you have it, sometimes you don't. Sometimes you're brilliant and relaxed; sometimes you can't get far enough away from that bumbling idiot you barely recognize as you. Wouldn't it be nice to have a set of tools so that when you are faced with the unexpected, you are calm and confident? You are equipped with default behavior that guides your conversation, your decision-making, and your behavior. You are ready for anything that comes your way. You welcome it even. Your spontaneous reaction is appropriate, timely, humorous, and innovative. You get to solutions that make you and your customer happy.

Let's revisit the scenarios. What if instead of hiding behind your desk, stumbling over your words, or sweating through your suit jacket, you were relaxed and playful? What if you could connect with the other person, reduce their stress, and find solutions together? In each of the scenarios, I'll play out just one example of what a credible response might look like. As with any creative process, there is certainly more than one right answer. Once you learn the tools, you will obviously find your own solutions, but this can get you started.

Scenario One

The shipment hasn't arrived. You look at the time again. It's 5 p.m. Jane Slidell, punctual as usual, rolls up in her Mercedes to inspect her order. The phone rings. You hear the supplier on the other end apologizing that the prototype for the solar panels, Jane Slidell's solar panels, will not be delivered. It's stuck somewhere in Tennessee. You watch her walk toward the door. What do you do?

Resolution One

Instead of thinking about yourself, wishing you weren't the one to have to explain to Jane, or steaming about the hold up, you focus on the customer. You ask yourself, "What is she feeling like? What is she expecting? How can I make her day great...and if not great, at least how can I help her to the best resolution so that she looks great in front of her 'customer?'" You know that's what is most important. Each of us has a "boss" of sorts; it is our customer.

You grab her file and walk confidently to meet her as she steps out of her car. Your smile tells her you're happy to see her and at her service. You note Jane's facial expression and nonverbal behavior. She appears weary from a long day in the car. Rather than start right in regurgitating what happened with the order, which is what would make you feel better, you do what would make Jane feel better. You ask her if she would like to step inside the air-conditioned office for a cup of coffee. You start with her creature comforts or at least you try to. But, Jane says no. She's had a long day, wants to see the order and get back on the road. Using the improvisational tool of "Yes, And! you acknowledge her long day and tell her you will do your best to get her on the road as quickly as possible.

You take the cue. You know just what she needs because you're focused on her. You tell it to her straight. You don't try to "cushion" the blow or make up excuses. So you say, "Jane, the order did not arrive from Tennessee. I'm sure you're frustrated. So am I. But, here's what I've done. I've talked to the supplier; I know you need those panels for the job site tomorrow. I will call first thing in the morning and get them to you. I will keep you informed as to their location and delivery time. My apologies. Now, the most important thing to me is to know how I can best help you deal with this. You're our best customer and you deserve the best service we can provide. Let's come up with the best solution together."

Notice you didn't make excuses. You didn't blame the problem on anyone else. You didn't try to get her to feel sorry for you, in fact you didn't call attention to yourself except to say, you would make it work, get it done. You didn't even give yourself an out by say, "I'll try my best," or some other lame deflective response. You take responsibility and you take action. You're honest, you anticipate her response, you stay calm rather than heighten the stress, and you're forward-thinking and solution-driven. She now knows she is not alone. You will see this through with her.

Scenario Two

"Is this thing on?" No. But you are. You're speaking to 1,500 people and the sound is out. Although you were promised the sound system would be working and you tested it yourself in rehearsal, it's clear that your first words to the 1,500 salespeople seated in front of you are clearly not being amplified. What do you do?

It's quite an honor to be asked and the president of the board just slipped into the back of the room. You are reviewing your notes one last time for your presentation at the regional trade show.

Resolution Two

You use the improvisational tool of staying in the moment. You can't change the sound system, make excuses, or postpone your presentation. So, what can you do? You can start out by recognizing what is in your favor. First, the audience. Audiences typically start out on your side. They walk in the door, most of the time, expecting good things. Otherwise, they would stay out in the hallway with the stale Danish. They've chosen to give you their time. They came to the trade show because they're interested in the product.

What else can you count on? Well, you know the technical crew is not going to abandon you. They don't want to look bad either. They know their job is to make you look good so, this is a great time to repay the favor. Help them out. The more gracious you are, the better. This only adds to the audience's positive feelings toward you.

You also know most of the people sitting in those chairs out there are terrified of speaking in front of a group. They are so relieved that it's you up there and not them that they automatically will be generous with you. Use this to your advantage, too.

Yes, it's true, this is scary. Yes, it could go badly. It's also true that "reality therapy" would tell us it is happening and you have to deal with it. There's no shrinking from this moment. If you're gracious and playful you'll come through this ahead. If you are tense, angry, and self-absorbed, it can go very badly. At this moment, everything is in your favor. Seize the opportunity.

Take a deep breath. Really deep. Walk on stage with confidence and the biggest smile you've ever had, not the fakey, bad family photo smile, a real genuine smile. Let them know that you're all in this together and this can be fun, funny even, rather than terrifying. You get to the lectern and, here's where your own ingenuity comes into play, you relax, look at your audience, and keep smiling. Keep looking. Keep smiling. Smile some more. Look at them. Take your time. Maybe you mouth a few words. Keep smiling and, the most magical thing will happen. They will start smiling, too. They will mirror you without even realizing it. They will smile back at you. They will also smile at each other, and then they will start laughing. They don't even know why they're laughing but they will. At the same time you're doing all this smiling, which will feel like forever, the tech crew will have had just enough time to get your mic working. They will give you the thumbs up. You will begin with a laughing relaxed crowd in front of you. Works every time.

Scenario Three

You have one chance to pitch that new project that would make your company a star. The CEO of one of your best customers has finally agreed to give you one hour of his time. You're wearing your best suit; you've had a good breakfast (eggs are "brain food" as your mother used to say so you've had two just in case). Unfortunately, just as you arrive, the CEO's receptionist tells you that his plans have changed and, much to his chagrin he says, he needs to reschedule. What do you do?

Resolution Three

You use the improvisational tool of focus. The reality here is that you can't change the amount of time you get with the CEO. It does you no good to pout. You really believe in this project, however, and you know if he doesn't hear about it now, you may not get a chance later. You reschedule if you can, but you know that's not enough. It can't wait that long.

You also know that he owes you one for this…not a lot, but something for cancelling at the last minute. You take advantage of that. You ask for one minute of his time…literally. The CEO will agree to this nine times out of 10 because he feels badly. But, when you say you need one minute of his time, you better mean it. The cool thing here is you do. You can pitch your project in one minute. He will be both surprised and impressed that you seized the moment and kept your word. I promise you, he won't forget the interchange.

If you've prepared properly for this presentation you know that you built your entire presentation around the one thing he needs to know. One thing. One tight memorable sentence that clearly identifies the "what" of the project and why it is important to him and the company. It's not about what you want to say but it's what he needs to know. It's all about him. All of it.

You walk into his office or ask to walk him to his next meeting and you remember that he is egocentric…like we all are. You tell him briefly and confidently the one thing he needs to know, thank him for his time, and tell him that you look forward to specifically identifying how this project will help the company once you have some more time together. You look him in the eye, smile, shake his hand and walk away. It's simple and powerful.

The art of improvisation provides the tools you need to think on your feet with deft intelligence, just when you need it. You still will need to plan and prepare but when you face the unexpected, you'll have the confidence and the tools to address it in a poised, professional, and even playful way.

A Way Of Life

This may be presumptuous. Pompous even. That's what happens when you've become entirely transformed by something. But since the day I experienced this stuff, my experiences have only deepened my awe for its power.

It's hard to capture something that's changed your life so dramatically in a few pages. I'm tempted to want to find a big barn, like Paul Sills did, and have us all bring our favorite snacks and improvise for days on end.

Certainly, I am a zealot on a large scale, using it to help merge company cultures in the midst of an acquisition or interrupt a destructive pattern in a product launch. But it also makes a difference in the way I handle an angry neighbor, engage in conversation around a fire, and talk to my nephew when he decided not to return to college for his junior year.

I no longer strive to be the loudest to be sure that everyone hears my idea. I relax when the group decides to go in a different direction that originally discussed. When a fire drill recently interrupted an already too brief two-hour workshop, we talked and played on our way to the "safe distance." Before I started improvising, that would have ruined my day.

I'm tempted to go on, but really, it's your turn. Reading about improvisation is the easy part. Now is the time to take the tools and make them your own.

At *The Second City*, someone would initiate a game. "Let's play Paper Chase." Someone else would jump in, "Oh you mean slips." A third would say, "Lines?" We may have called the game different names. It didn't matter. We just started to play.

Not too long after, the next level to the game would come. "What if we only asked the audience to give us secrets?" or "How about if we are at a staff meeting and you can only grab a line of dialogue when you find a reason to stand up. You have to justify it of course." Or "Maybe we can use the slips of dialogue to respond as an expert with the audience acting like they are interviewing the expert for a job opening."

In other words, we became an ensemble first. We solidified the trust by playing through the games together. Finally, we'd take the games and make them our own. You are invited to do the same. Find an ensemble or accept the one you have. Learn the tools of improvisation together. Start using them as a part of your brainstorming, meetings, and presentations. Use them to deal with conflict. Find ways to make each other laugh.

And then, move to the next level. Morph them to fit your situation. With your customer in mind, shape your use of the tools to help you connect on the showroom floor, in the cafeteria, and at the dealership.

Engage those around you in a daily dance of "Yes, And!" And use the other tools of focus, in the moment, who/what/where, give and take, and commit to improvise your way to creating a new day.

Use them to help you move past daily survival, past your heart racing from one urgent call for help to the next resignation that forces you to settle for less. Instead, put on the tools; wear them around until it's no longer a conscious choice. Start to experience the energy that comes with thriving. And, as your shoulders relax and you start laughing more, take note.

Allow yourself and your team to evolve in ways that result in the kind of collective response Friedman champions in his book, *That Used To Be Us*. I repeat his call to us, "Wake up! Pay attention! The world you are living in has fundamentally changed. It is not the world you think it is. You need to adapt because the health, security and future of the country depend on it."[23]

Clearly then, the health, security, and future of your company depend on it as well.

---

[23]   Friedman, Thomas L. *That Used to Be Us: How America Fell Behind in the World It Invented and How We Can Come Back*. 2011. Macmillan.

LIVE IT

Pause.

Find your focus in the moment.

Settle yourself.

Pay attention to the people around you.
They are a gift to you in this moment.

Discover the what.
Sometimes it's spoken, easy to find.
Most times, it's unspoken and requires a deeper listening.

Soak in your surroundings — their influence on who and what.

YES, AND! the focus, the moment, the
who, the what, and the where.
Find ways to get to agreement.

Recognize that getting to agreement is not a destination.
It is a way station on your journey.
It is one moment, one decision, and one idea building on the next.

Give and take.
Not everything has to go your way.

Try a different way.

Contribute and then make room for someone else to contribute.

Commit to remaining focused, staying in the moment, experiencing the who/what/where, to YES, AND!..., to give and take.

And then, do it all over again...

Until the cycle is seamless, second nature.

Continue until the behaviors become as natural as breathing.

Special Thanks to

All the people who taught me, gave me gifts on stage and off, who have been patient, encouraging, and made me laugh.

To my family, each of whom has yes anded me in profound ways despite all my shortcomings. I love you all for that. To the Second City folks who formalized the yesanding and honored me by inviting me in to the family, namely Andrew Alexander, Kelly Leonard and Lyn O'Kersse. To Rico Bruce Wade, our producer/director and those I had the good fortune to play with including Eric Black, Larry Campbell, Margaret (Exner) Edwartowski, John Edwartowski, Kirk Hanley, Elaine Hendriks, Keegan-Michael Key, Joe Latessa, Nyima Woods (Funk), Joshua Funk, Michael Gellman, Andrew Graham, Marc Evan Jackson, Brandon Johnson, Antoine McKay, Maribeth Monroe, Mary Vinette, Marc Warzecha, Ron West, and Catherine Worth.

And, to all the companies who opened their doors to let Fishladder Inc. come in and play. To my friend Liz Appold who spent seven years by my side in the office.

On the manuscript, special thanks go to my father, for his playful illustrations and spirit. To two of my sisters, Kathy and Susan Pories, who helped me, unearth the structure by doing what only sisters can do. To my Writers Group - Jean Reed Bahle, Debra Freeberg, Catherine Frerichs, Margery Guest, Hillary Harper, Diane Herbruck, Jill Hinton, and Marti Ayres White - for endless support, insight, and cups of tea. To Dan Hawkins who gave me a hug and handed me scissors. And to Carrie Thrall, who put every hair in place with her fine tooth comb and did so with a smile on her face.

And to Rhonda Lubberts for her gracious patience in her unofficial role as master of ceremonies, event coordinator, marketing guru, chief supporter, and soul mate.

Index